**Mad River, Marjorie Rowland,
and the Quest for LGBTQ
Teachers' Rights**

New Directions in the History of Education

Series editor, Benjamin Justice

The New Directions in the History of Education series seeks to publish innovative books that push the traditional boundaries of the history of education. Topics may include social movements in education; the history of cultural representations of schools and schooling; the role of public schools in the social production of space; and the perspectives and experiences of African Americans, Latinx Americans, women, queer folk, and others. The series will take a broad, inclusive look at American education in formal settings, from prekindergarten to higher education, as well as in out-of-school and informal settings. We also invite historical scholarship that informs and challenges popular conceptions of educational policy and policy making and that addresses questions of social justice, equality, democracy, and the formation of popular knowledge.

Dionne Danns, *Crossing Segregated Boundaries: Remembering Chicago School Desegregation*

Sharon S. Lee, *An Unseen Unheard Minority: Asian American Students at the University of Illinois*

Margaret A. Nash and Karen Graves, *Mad River, Marjorie Rowland, and the Quest for LGBTQ Teachers' Rights*

Diana D'Amico Pawlewicz, *Blaming Teachers: Professionalization Policies and the Failure of Reform in American History*

Kyle P. Steele, *Making a Mass Institution: Indianapolis and the American High School*

Mad River, Marjorie Rowland, and the Quest for LGBTQ Teachers' Rights

MARGARET A. NASH AND KAREN L. GRAVES

Rutgers University Press

New Brunswick, Camden, and Newark, New Jersey, and London

978-1-9788-2751-6 (cloth)
978-1-9788-2750-9 (paper)
978-1-9788-2752-3 (e-pub)

Cataloging-in-publication data is available from the Library of Congress.
LCCN 2021050027

A British Cataloging-in-Publication record for this book is available from the British Library.

References to internet websites (URLs) were accurate at the time of writing. Neither the author nor Rutgers University Press is responsible for URLs that may have expired or changed since the manuscript was prepared.

Chapter 1 adapted with permission from Graves, K., Nash, M. A. (2018). Staking a Claim in Mad River: Advancing Civil Rights for Queer America. In D. A. Santoro & L. Cain (Eds.), *Principled Resistance: How Teachers Resolve Ethical Dilemmas*, pp. 171–185. Cambridge, MA: Harvard Education Press. Copyright © 2018 The President and Fellows of Harvard College.

♾ The paper used in this publication meets the requirements of the American National Standard for Information Sciences—Permanence of Paper for Printed Library Materials, ANSI Z39.48-1992.

www.rutgersuniversitypress.org

Manufactured in the United States of America

Dedicated to Marjorie Rowland and to all the brave
LGBTQ educators, past and present.

There is no possible conflict between the interest of the child and the interest of the teacher. . . . For both the child and the teacher freedom is the condition of development. The atmosphere in which it is easiest to teach is the atmosphere in which it is easiest to learn. The same things that are a burden to the teacher are a burden also to the child. The same things which restrict her powers restrict his powers also.

—**MARGARET A. HALEY**, 1904

Contents

Preface

In 1974, a high school principal asked a guidance counselor who identified as bisexual to resign. She refused, confident that she was good at her job, that she helped students, and that the principal was wrong to ask her to resign simply because of her sexuality. Eventually a jury and some judges agreed with her, but a majority of judges did not. The counselor, Marjorie Rowland, lost her job and never worked in a school setting again.

Rowland's story took place outside of Dayton, Ohio, but it could have happened almost anywhere. It *did* happen almost anywhere, for decades, including in the present day. Unbeknownst to Rowland, other educators were facing similar situations. Some of them took their cases to court, while others did not have the financial or emotional resources to fight what seemed like an inevitably losing battle. Rowland did choose to fight, backed with the institutional support of the National Education Association, which had just recently included sexual orientation in its category of protected groups. Her case is important, not just because she chose to pursue justice but because it led to a written statement by U.S. Supreme Court Justice William Brennan. While Brennan's statement changed nothing for Rowland, it became a foundation for other civil rights cases for LGBTQ people. This book is the story of what happened to Marjorie Rowland, how it happened, and why it matters.

LGBTQ people have made great gains toward social, political, and legal equality in recent years, and these gains are to be celebrated. But there also have been tremendous backlash, targeted violence, and some erosion of rights. Teachers have often been the lightning rod for attacks against LGBTQ people, as many anti-LGBTQ crusades have taken cover under the guise of protecting children. This book recounts some of the history of those battles and suggests that LGBTQ people will not have full equality until LGBTQ educators are fully accepted in schoolhouses across the country.

Mad River, Marjorie Rowland, and the Quest for LGBTQ Teachers' Rights

1

Staking a Claim in Mad River

It is fair to say that discrimination against homosexuals is "likely . . . to reflect deep-seated prejudice rather than . . . rationality."

Lesbian, gay, bisexual, and transgender (LGBT) teachers have fought for their rights for a long time.[1] For most of the twentieth century, any hint of same-sex desire or departure from binary gender norms could imperil the social standing, employment, housing options, freedom, and very lives of all LGBT people in the United States, including educators. But teachers have evoked a particular animosity from antigay activists. Because of teachers' work with vulnerable children, because of teachers serving as role models in classrooms and communities, and because of homophobic rhetoric that falsely equates gayness with pedophilia, LGBT teachers have sometimes borne the brunt of antigay campaigns. LGBT teachers have suffered taunts and torments; have faced interrogations, arrests, and death threats; and have lost not only their jobs but their beloved professions and their livelihoods. For decades, school officials charged educators with immoral and unprofessional conduct simply on the basis of their LGBT status and deemed them in violation of moral turpitude clauses in state education codes.

Beginning in the 1960s a few embattled educators demanded their day in court, seeking the right to remain in the profession they loved. In 1969 the Supreme Court of California found that homosexual conduct did not make a person "unfit" for teaching. A few years later, in the state of Oregon, Peggy Burton became the first LGBT teacher to bring a federal civil rights suit for undue dismissal. A district court struck down the immorality statute that school officials had used to fire her, finding it unconstitutionally vague. Throughout the next decade, courts across the country issued a patchwork of opinions on equal employment claims brought by LGBT educators, tacking back and forth between broadening and limiting rights. The Fourth Circuit Court held that gay teachers did not have to stay in the closet to keep their jobs, but the Supreme Court of Washington ruled that teachers could be fired simply for their LGBT status. A New Jersey court decided that local school boards maintained wide latitude in determining whether LGBT teachers were fit to teach. The Sixth Circuit Court struck down a lower court ruling that LGBT teachers could rely on freedom of speech and equal protection claims in defense of their jobs. For decades the U.S. Supreme Court remained silent on this issue, denying every petition to hear cases brought by fired LGBT workers, including four cases brought by educators.

In a historic ruling announced on June 14, 2020, the U.S. Supreme Court held that Title VII of the Civil Rights Act of 1964 prohibits discrimination against LGBT employees. Seventeen years after *Lawrence v. Texas*, the ruling that struck down sodomy laws branding LGBT people as criminals, and five years after *Obergefell v. Hodges*, the ruling that struck down prohibitions on same-sex marriage, the court determined in *Bostock v. Clayton County* that Title VII's provision against firing employees "because of sex" applies to gay and transgender workers. The victory of *Bostock* built on the work of many courageous educators who fought for employment rights for LGBT people. In this volume we address an important legal case in the history of LGBT educators' struggle for employment, a case that almost no one has heard of.

Marjorie Rowland v. Mad River School District involves a guidance counselor in Dayton, Ohio, who was fired by her school district in 1974 for being bisexual. Her case made it to the U.S. Supreme Court, but the Supreme Court justices declined to consider it. In a spectacular published dissent, Justice Brennan laid out the arguments for why the First and Fourteenth

Amendments applied to gays and lesbians. Brennan's *Rowland* dissent has been a foundation for a number of critical LGBT civil rights cases since then. Sadly, a Supreme Court majority has yet to recognize the constitutional claims brought on behalf of LGBT public employees. In *Bostock*, the conservative Roberts court provided a different pathway to equal employment for LGBT workers at large through its reading of Title VII of the Civil Rights Act. While the decision clearly was a victory for LGBT people, time will tell how permanent or solid this victory is. As legal scholars point out, "sexual orientation" and "gender identity" "still fail to appear in the text of Title VII." LGBT concerns were instead subsumed under the heading of "sex," and so LGBT protection from discrimination comes in the form of "a technicality . . . rather [than] as a consequence of straightforwardly recognizing their rights to full and equal citizenship."[2]

Although the victory for LGBT workers eventually came through a different route than that pursued by educators and other government employees on constitutional grounds, their collective efforts no doubt wore away at the homophobic prejudice that defined the legal landscape for many years. Furthermore, Marjorie Rowland's legal struggle remains an important example of agency and action in an educator occupying a vulnerable social position.

This chapter provides an overview of LGBT educator history and describes court cases that happened before and during Rowland's legal battles. We then introduce Rowland's case briefly and discuss the importance of the dissent issued when her case made it to the U.S. Supreme Court. With this background established, chapter 2, "'I Had to Be the Fighter,'" tells Rowland's story in depth. We discuss how the arguments in the case were framed differently at each level and examine the backgrounds of the judges who made the decisions. We also discuss the implications for Rowland's professional life: her difficulty finding a job after being dismissed as a guidance counselor, her challenges supporting herself and her three small children, and her response to the long-lasting political repercussions of the case, including additional charges that a prosecutor lobbed against her.

Chapter 3, "The Meaning of *Mad River*: Implications of the Case," explores two aspects of how courts have since encountered the case. First, Brennan's dissent has helped build a legal foundation for LGBT rights. We trace the impact of his dissent in later cases. Second, because *Rowland v. Mad River* rested on issues of freedom of speech, the case has had implications for academic freedom. We discuss those here as well.

By the 1990s, some LGBT teachers began to organize and to insist on visibility. One marker of this movement was the book *Coming Out of the Classroom Closet*, published in 1992, which publicized issues and concerns for LGBT teachers and students. The Gay Lesbian Straight Education Network (GLSEN) formed, further advancing the mobilization of teachers. Chapter 4, "'Coming Out of the Classroom Closet': LGBT Teachers' Lives after *Mad River*," examines LGBT teachers' lives in these decades.

Finally, in chapter 5, "Movements Forward and Back," we look at the status of LGBTQ teachers and students today. Many gains have been made; visibility for both teachers and students is more possible than it was in Marjorie Rowland's days at Mad River. Many states and cities have protections for LGBTQ students, and some states have protections for LGBTQ teachers that preceded the 2020 *Bostock* decision. As of 2021, five states require public schools to teach an LGBTQ-inclusive curriculum: California, New Jersey, Colorado, Oregon, and Illinois.[3] Yet there continue to be many challenges, especially in the aftermath of a presidential administration that eroded rights for transgender people, both in the military and in schools. Department of Education (DOE) secretary Betsy DeVos reduced the impact of Title IX, which was one of the few avenues for protection for LGBTQ students, directed the DOE to retreat from investigating complaints from transgender students regarding access to bathrooms and locker rooms, and forced schools to rescind transgender-inclusive policies in athletic programs.[4] As federal, state, and school district LGBTQ policies ebb and flow, it is important to remember the example that Marjorie Rowland set, at a much different time, regarding the protection of civil liberties for teachers and their students.

Charting Political Currents against LGBT Educators

School districts did not always hound LGBT teachers out of the classroom. In fact, intolerance for LGBT teachers did not begin in earnest until the mid-twentieth century. As Jackie Blount shows in her watershed publication, *Fit to Teach*, scholarly literature as well as elements in early twentieth-century popular culture contributed to the slowly developing backlash against LGBT teachers. As late as 1929 it was possible for the prominent researcher Katherine Bement Davis to publish *Factors in the Sex Life of Twenty-Two Hundred Women*. Teachers and superintendents constituted just over half of the twelve hundred single, college-educated women in the study. Among these educators, 22 percent reported experiencing intense emotional relations with women, and another 25 percent reported experiencing intense sexual relations with women. Davis's study marked the end of a period when candid discussion of one's sexual expression was possible, however. By 1932 Willard Waller's popular text *The Sociology of Teaching* warned against employing homosexual teachers, claiming that homosexuality was contagious.[5]

At the end of World War II, Cold War politics framed the most repressive period in U.S. history for gay and lesbian citizens, and educators became a particularly vulnerable target. One reason for the increased repression was the increased visibility of homosexuality. Alfred Kinsey published his famous study *The Sexual Behavior of the Human Male* in 1948, documenting that more than a third of the men in his study had had at least one homosexual experience.[6] Many civic leaders and citizens were horrified and pushed for more punitive laws that often included a psychiatric diagnosis. In some states, by law, if you had homosexual tendencies, whether or not you had engaged in homosexual behavior, you were labeled a sexual psychopath.[7] As a result, this period was marked by a widespread purge of gay and lesbian teachers, professors, and students. The most relentless attack occurred in Florida during the Johns Committee investigations.[8] Between 1957 and 1963 the state investigative committee actively pursued lesbian and gay schoolteachers, subjected them to interrogation, fired them from teaching positions, and revoked their professional credentials. By 1963 the committee reported that it had revoked seventy-one teachers' certificates with sixty-three cases pending and had files on another hundred "suspects."[9] A combination of factors led to the committee's demise in 1965, but, as Stacy Braukman shows, the ideology that powered its crusade simply went underground. A 1977 reprisal in Miami pushed Florida to the center of the national spotlight on the gay rights movement.[10]

Some communities in the United States began to inch toward civil rights protections for gay and lesbian citizens in the 1970s, overturning sodomy laws and prohibiting job discrimination.[11] This political action triggered antigay organizing by conservative political groups. Among all public employees protected by newly minted antidiscrimination laws, lesbian and gay schoolteachers drew the most contentious reaction. In 1977 and 1978 national attention was riveted on the gay rights battles taking place in Miami and California.[12] In Florida, activists challenged a law that protected gay men and lesbians from discrimination in employment, housing, and public accommodations, strategically narrowing the scope of the referendum to focus on gay and lesbian teachers. In California, the referendum was based entirely on the question of who could teach in public schools.

The Florida referendum was a resounding defeat for the gay rights movement. Reporters characterized the vote as a "stunning setback" for gay rights activists that would reverberate across the nation.[13] It was followed by similar retrenchment in Minnesota, Kansas, and Oregon. Clearly, the political tide had turned, making the 1978 statewide vote in California increasingly important. There, gay rights groups organized effectively while antigay forces overextended their political reach, targeting all teachers who supported gay rights. This time voters rejected the referendum, handing the gay rights movement a critical victory.

At the same time, however, the state senator Mary Helm introduced a bill in Oklahoma that was a virtual twin of the California law. It passed in the lower house by a vote of 88–2 without debate and was approved in the state senate unanimously. The new law allowed school districts in Oklahoma to fire gay men, lesbians, and any other educator who engaged in "public homosexual conduct," defined broadly as "advocating, soliciting, imposing, encouraging or promoting public or private homosexual activity in a manner that creates a substantial risk that such conduct will come to the attention of schoolchildren or school employees."[14] In other words, the law prohibited teachers from supporting gay rights. The National Gay Task Force (NGTF) challenged the law on multiple grounds: that it violated freedom of speech, freedom of association, freedom of religion, the right to privacy, the equal protection clause of the Fourteenth Amendment, and the fact that the law was too vague and too broad. A federal district judge upheld the law, and the case went to the Tenth Circuit Court on appeal. In a 2–1 decision, the appellate court struck down the part of the law that restricted free speech. The dissenting judge James Barrett was furious, writing that a teacher who advocated on behalf of gay rights was less deserving of constitutional protection than one who advocated "violence, sabotage and terrorism."[15]

When the case reached the U.S. Supreme Court, six justices voted to hear the case. The court had a history of turning away cases brought by gay citizens who wanted to claim civil rights. In this case, the appellate court's decision in favor of gay rights advocates would stand unless the Supreme Court ruled otherwise. *Board of Education v. National Gay Task Force* thus became the first Supreme Court case to address gay and lesbian teachers. Due to Justice Lewis Powell's absence, the decision was tied 4–4, meaning that the NGTF victory at the appellate court was affirmed. The part of the law that infringed teachers' freedom of speech was ruled unconstitutional.

Prior to the political organizing in Florida, California, and Oklahoma, individual teachers had begun challenging dismissals based on their sexual orientation in court. Backed first by the American Civil Liberties Union (ACLU) and then the National Education Association (NEA), plaintiffs fighting for their jobs tested legal arguments designed to keep LGBT educators out of schools. These early decisions turned on morality and privacy assumptions that had long circumscribed all teachers' autonomy and employment rights. In some cases, teachers gained ground in the effort to secure nondiscriminatory employment protections, but, as Jackie Blount has observed, in all cases the individual teachers whose jobs were on the line were displaced.[16]

Three of these cases reached the Supreme Court. In 1972 Joseph Acanfora was completing his student teaching assignment at Penn State when, as part of a news story on the university's gay student group, he noted that he was gay. College officials subjected him to intense scrutiny regarding his character before forwarding his application for a teaching certificate to the state department of education. Acanfora accepted a job teaching eighth-grade science in Montgomery County, Maryland. About a month into the school year, the Pennsylvania Department of Education held a news conference, announcing it was approving Acanfora's request for a teaching certificate; Acanfora's principal promptly removed him from his teaching duties. Although there was strong community support for Acanfora, the district court handed down a mixed opinion. It protected homosexuals' right to teach but noted that Acanfora had violated the "duty of privacy" he was to maintain as a public schoolteacher. The Fourth Circuit Court of Appeals rejected that reasoning and upheld Acanfora's right to freedom of speech. But it held that his dismissal could stand, given that he had failed to list his membership in the student group Homophiles of Penn State on his job application. The Supreme Court denied a petition for writ of certiorari (cert.) in October 1974, and Acanfora left teaching.[17]

In October 1977 the Supreme Court denied cert. in two more cases: *Gish v. Board of Education of the Borough of Paramus* and *Gaylord v. Tacoma School District No. 10*. James Gaylord, a Phi Beta Kappa graduate of the University of Washington, was a high school history teacher who had established a strong record of teaching over a twelve-year period. He had not disclosed information about his sexual orientation and was not charged with any sort of immoral conduct, but when his vice principal asked if he was gay, he said yes. Gaylord was fired in December 1972 on charges of "immorality." The Supreme Court of Washington upheld the dismissal on the basis of Gaylord's status as a gay man, a ruling the U.S. Supreme Court did not review.[18]

That same day, the court denied cert. in *Gish*. In 1972 veteran high school English teacher John Gish organized the Gay Teachers Caucus of the NEA. Later that year, the Paramus, New Jersey, school board ordered Gish to take a psychiatric examination. Gish refused. Supported by the ACLU, he began a five-year legal journey that ended when the Supreme Court refused to hear the case, leaving the New Jersey Superior Court's decision intact. Relying on the 1952 *Adler v. Board of Education of the City of New York* ruling that had since been superseded, the New Jersey court found that school boards maintained wide latitude in determining the fitness of teachers. They considered Gish's "actions in support of 'gay' rights" a deviation from "normal mental health which might affect his ability to teach, discipline, and associate with students."[19]

Each of these cases had been set in motion in 1972, just as the gay rights movement was gaining traction. Over the course of the decade, two lines of argument emerged, anchored in the First Amendment freedom of speech and the Fourteenth Amendment equal protection clauses. By the time the Supreme Court had its next opportunity to weigh in on the matter of employment rights for gay and lesbian teachers, Justice Brennan was fed up with the court's persistent refusal to consider the important constitutional questions at stake. In 1985 he issued a dissent in *Rowland v. Mad River Local School Dist.* that would provide an important foundation for legal breakthroughs in the future.[20] More than a decade had passed since Rowland made the decision to claim her rights.

Turmoil in Mad River: Rowland's Resistance and Brennan's Dissent

Marjorie Rowland began work as a counselor at Stebbins High School in Dayton, Ohio, in August 1974. In November, she told her secretary that two particular students did not need to have special permission to see her

Major LGBTQ Court Cases

Date	Case	Summary
1974 Supreme Court denies cert.	*Acanfora v. Board of Education*	Maryland teacher fired for prior membership in a college homophile club. Circuit court rules that schools cannot fire teachers on the basis of homosexuality, but he still lost his job because he did not list club membership on his teaching application.
1977 Supreme Court denies cert.	*Gaylord v. Tacoma School District No. 10*	Washington State teacher fired for homosexual *identity* (rather than behavior). State Supreme Court agrees that his identity was reason enough to be barred from teaching.
1977 Supreme Court denies cert.	*Gish v. Board of Education of the Borough of Paramus*	Teacher fired for refusing school district order to take a psychiatric exam after helping organize the Gay Teachers Caucus of the NEA. New Jersey Superior Court rules that school districts retain wide latitude in determining one's fitness to teach.
1985 Supreme Court denies cert.	*Rowland v. Mad River School District*	U.S. Supreme Court refuses to hear Rowland's case, but Brennan writes his landmark dissent.
1985	*Board of Education of Oklahoma City v. National Gay Task Force*	U.S. Supreme Court upholds Oklahoma law allowing school districts to ban LGB teachers, but districts cannot ban teachers from talking about LGB issues.
1986	*Bowers v. Hardwick*	U.S. Supreme Court decides that states can make sex between same-sex consenting adults illegal; sexual activity for LGB people is criminal if a state deems it so (many states did).
1996	*Romer v. Evans*	U.S. Supreme Court rules that "equal protection under the law" applies to homosexuals.
1996	*Nabozny v. Podlesny*	Seventh Circuit Court holds public school districts and officials liable for failing to protect students from homophobic assault.
2003	*Lawrence v. Texas*	U.S. Supreme Court rules that sodomy laws are unconstitutional. LGB sex is no longer a felony. Overturns *Bowers*.
2013	*United States v. Windsor*	U.S. Supreme Court determines that the federal government must recognize same-sex marriages that have been approved by the states.

(continued)

Major LGBTQ Court Cases (continued)

Date	Case	Summary
2015	*Obergefell v. Hodges*	U.S. Supreme Court determines that state governments cannot ban same-sex marriage. Marriage is a fundamental right.
2020	*Bostock v. Clayton County*	U.S. Supreme Court rules that the Title VII (of the Civil Rights Act) ban on workplace discrimination based on sex includes LGBT workers.

and that if Rowland was available, the secretary should allow either of those students to come in. The reason, Rowland disclosed in confidence, was that each of these students had come out to their parents as gay, the parents had not responded well, and the students needed support. The secretary peppered Rowland with questions, leading to Rowland saying that she was bisexual and was currently in love with a woman.[21]

The secretary told a supervisor and the school principal that Rowland was bisexual. When Rowland refused to resign, she was called to a meeting with the superintendent. Supported by an ACLU attorney and a teacher's union representative, Rowland again refused to resign and was immediately suspended. When a federal judge blocked the suspension, district officials reassigned her to a job where she would have no contact with students. At the end of the year, Mad River School District did not renew Rowland's contract.[22]

Like other gay and lesbian teachers fighting for their jobs, Rowland experienced the loss of career and income, received threatening and obscene phone calls, and went bankrupt as her case made its way through the lower courts. In 1981 a district court jury found that Rowland's equal protection and free speech rights had been violated. In 1984 a divided Sixth Circuit Court overturned the ruling. Chief Judge Pierce Lively dismissed First Amendment protections because he determined that Rowland's speech did not address "matters of public concern." The equal protection claim fell victim to the court's opinion that there was no evidence that Rowland had been treated differently than heterosexuals.[23] Rowland then appealed to the U.S. Supreme Court.

It takes four justices to move a case forward at the Supreme Court. With the support of Brennan and Marshall alone on *Rowland v. Mad River*, the court was giving its "usual silent treatment to [a] . . . case that might have changed the status quo," observers noted.[24] But this time, Brennan took the opportunity to issue a blistering dissent, joined by Marshall. Brennan framed the case as a question of the constitutional rights of public employees to maintain and express their private sexual preferences. Since the lower courts were in disarray on this point, he argued, it was time for the Supreme Court to address the issue. Brennan noted that the facts uncovered at the jury trial were clear. Rowland had been dismissed solely because she told a secretary and some fellow teachers about her bisexual status. This speech did not in any way interfere with her proper performance of duties or the regular operation of the school. The dismissal was a violation of Rowland's free speech rights in accordance with the Pickering standard and her Fourteenth Amendment right to equal protection under the law.

Brennan was clearly irritated with the Sixth Circuit Court of Appeals ruling that Rowland's speech was not protected because it was not a matter of public concern, and he noted that the lower court dismissed Rowland's equal protection claim in error, without citing precedent. He launched into his analysis of the case with this parting shot regarding the circuit court's "crabbed reading of our precedents and unexplained disregard of the jury and judge's factual findings. Because they are so patently erroneous, these maneuvers suggest only a desire to evade the central question: may a State dismiss a public employee based on her bisexual status alone?"[25]

Brennan wrote that Rowland's case raised a substantial First Amendment claim. It was settled law that a state cannot condition public employment on a basis that infringes on free speech. The circuit court had cited *Connick v. Myers*, 461 U.S. 138 (1983), to uphold Rowland's dismissal, claiming that her speech did not address a "matter of political, social, or other concern to the community."[26] Brennan raised two objections: Rowland's speech *did* address a matter of public concern, and even if that were not the case, the Pickering-Connick rationale would apply. That standard seeks to balance "the interest of public employees in speaking freely and that of public employers in operating their workplaces without disruption."[27] Since Rowland had not disrupted the school environment, her speech was protected. Brennan concluded that it was "an entirely harmless mention of a fact" that "apparently triggered certain prejudices held by her supervisors."[28]

While the school disruption test is standard practice in free speech cases involving teachers and students, Brennan's affirmation that Rowland's speech addressed a matter of public concern advanced public rhetoric in support of gay rights. Brennan suggested a parallel with racial discrimination, writing, "I think it impossible not to note that a similar public debate is

currently ongoing regarding the rights of homosexuals. The fact of peti-
tioner's bisexuality, once spoken, necessarily and ineluctably involved
her in that debate. Speech that 'touches upon' this explosive issue is no less
deserving of constitutional attention than speech relating to more widely
condemned forms of discrimination."[29]

Brennan then turned to Fourteenth Amendment equal protection considerations, arguing that discrimination against homosexuals and bisexuals
might well meet the standards for establishing a "suspect class" or be found
to impinge on fundamental rights. He recognized that homosexuals constituted a "significant and insular minority" of the population and suggested
that they met the criteria for strict scrutiny. "Because of the immediate and
severe opprobrium often manifested against homosexuals once so identified
publicly, members of this group are particularly powerless to pursue their
rights openly in the political arena. Moreover, homosexuals have historically been the object of pernicious and sustained hostility, and it is fair to
say that discrimination against homosexuals is 'likely . . . to reflect deep-
seated prejudice rather than . . . rationality.'"[30]

Brennan argued that discrimination based on one's sexuality had
already been found by some courts to infringe on fundamental constitutional rights, such as privacy and freedom of expression. Although he
believed that many precedents support the argument that public employees have a fundamental right to "private choices involving family life and
personal autonomy," the Supreme Court had not yet weighed in on such
questions.[31] Brennan's 1985 dissent stands today as the first of the most critical gay rights statements issued by any justice, alongside Justice Anthony
Kennedy's majority opinions in *Lawrence v. Texas* 539 U.S. 558 (2003) and
Obergefell v. Hodges 576 U.S. ___ (2015) and Justice Neil Gorsuch's majority
opinion in *Bostock v. Clayton County* 590 U.S. ___ (2020).

Conclusion

Marjorie Rowland stood in a long line of LGBT educators expelled from
the teaching profession on the basis of professional standards warped by
homophobia. While individual teachers found limited avenues for resisting
the teacher purges of the early Cold War period (for example, guarding the
details of their personal lives, avoiding social gatherings, remaining silent,
or stonewalling when questioned), Rowland belonged to the generation

who leveraged the law to challenge their dismissals publicly.[32] The option was not feasible before 1964, the year the ACLU reversed its position to supporting LGBT citizens in discrimination cases. The NEA began providing support for LGBT teachers fighting for their jobs in 1974, the year Mad River School District suspended Rowland. It was not until the 2003 *Lawrence v. Texas* decision that educators in all states could work relatively free of the fear of losing their credentials as statutory felons, simply due to LGBT status. And it took the nation another thirty-five years after Rowland's Supreme Court petition was denied to extend equal employment protection to all LGBT workers.[33]

Although generally unacknowledged in LGBT histories, the resistance of Rowland and the other educators who demanded their day in court advanced both the LGBT movement and the democratic principles that define American schooling at its best. Brennan's dissent in *Rowland v. Mad River Local School District* has been cited in over thirty opinions, including *United States v. Windsor.*[34] Essentially, he laid the foundation for First and Fourteenth Amendment claims that later courts used to realize civil rights for LGBT Americans. Known as the "conscience of the Court," Brennan was a stalwart protector of individual rights. "Brennan believed that majorities could take care of themselves through the legislative process. He was less convinced that solitary human beings, particularly those marginalized by society, could do so."[35] Justice Thurgood Marshall was the only other justice to join the dissent.

At the time few others could appreciate these LGBT educators' commitment to the enduring ideals of democratic education. Instead, LGBT teachers were the dominant ideology's version of a triple threat—perceived as dangerous to children and youth because of an assumed pathological, sinful, and criminal nature. Relatively few could see beyond these destructive assumptions that were only just beginning to crumble. As workers in the public sphere who are called on to guard the nation's most cherished principles, all teachers fall under strict public scrutiny. As the gay rights movement was getting underway, LGBT teachers found themselves with a significant role to play, both in the movement and in their profession.

At the core of citizenship education in the United States is the teacher's responsibility not only to ensure that students' rights are protected but also to protect their own constitutional rights, setting an example for interpreting the meaning of civil liberties. Here the democratic meets the pedagogical principle. Earlier in the twentieth century, Justice Felix Frankfurter famously called teachers the "high priests of democracy," whose job it is "to foster those habits of open-mindedness and critical inquiry which alone make for responsible citizens, who, in turn, make possible an enlightened and effective public opinion."[36] The legal battles that Marjorie Rowland and countless others waged provide an important lesson for the generations that followed.

Of course, when it all began, Marjorie Rowland had no idea that her name would be attached to a decision that had this impact. She had no idea that she would be involved in a lawsuit at all. Back in the fall of 1974, she was simply a guidance counselor beginning a new job. It is to her story we now turn.

2

"I Had to Be the Fighter"

I just knew something was up, because there was a hush around the secretary's office, which was outside of my office.

Marjorie Rowland was an unlikely hero. Born and raised near Toledo, Ohio, she was a good student who attended church regularly and chose to be baptized as a teenager. She attended college at Wittenberg University in Springfield, Ohio, and graduated in 1962 with a license to teach. In her first year of teaching, she met another new teacher, and soon the two married. Over the next several years, the couple added three children to their family. The marriage ended in 1971, leaving Rowland with three small children to support as a single parent. She was a young woman with serious responsibilities.

And she was a young woman who could be sexually and emotionally attracted to both women and men.

In the summer of 1974, she earned a master's degree in counseling and that August was hired as a guidance counselor at a high school in the Mad River School District in Dayton, Ohio. Today the Mad River website includes the sentence "Applicants are considered for all positions without regard to race, color, religion, sex (including gender identity, sexual orientation, and pregnancy), national origin, age, disability, or genetic information."[1]

But in 1974, there was no such policy of protection regarding sexual orientation (or, likely, many of the other categories).

Dayton was a midsized city in southwestern Ohio, with a population then of about 200,000.[2] Wilbur and Orville Wright, inventors of the airplane, came from Dayton, as did the African American poet Paul Laurence Dunbar; the three attended high school together and published a newspaper together.[3] Industry was an important part of the city. Manufacturing included farming tools and equipment and cash registers. Dayton also had a role in the Manhattan Project and received $1.7 billion in defense contracts during the war.[4] Researchers in Dayton worked on refining polonium for use as triggering devices for the atomic bomb.[5] Wright-Patterson Air Force Base, established in 1917, plays a prominent role in Dayton. During World War II, the base employed as many as 50,000 people. During subsequent wars, the base was the site of the Air Technical Intelligence Centers and Air Force Technical Intelligence Schools. Until 1975, the base was home to the Seventeenth Bombardment Wing, responsible for training intelligence personnel in all branches of the armed forces.[6] Dayton, then, was a city of industry, manufacturing, and the military.

Rowland worked in Dayton, but she lived in Yellow Springs, a village of several thousand people just twenty miles away. Yellow Springs's history was quite different from Dayton's. The village was founded in the early nineteenth century by acolytes of Robert Owen, the founder of the famous utopian community at New Harmony, Indiana. Although the Yellow Springs version of New Harmony did not last long, the village continued to have a counterculture ethos. In the mid-nineteenth century, it became home to Antioch College, whose first president, a Unitarian, was the well-known school reformer Horace Mann. A later president, Arthur Morgan, was a Quaker and founder of intentional Quaker communities. During the Red Scare of the 1950s, Yellow Springs and Antioch College were targeted for questioning because of the prevalence of left-leaning politics among residents. During the 1960s and 1970s, Yellow Springs and Antioch were actively engaged in the civil rights movement.[7] This was where Rowland chose to live, and it was this sensibility regarding social justice that she took with her to her job in the Mad River School District.

That autumn of 1974, in her first few months on the job as a counselor at the high school, Rowland talked to lots of students about lots of things: career paths, college opportunities, and teenage life issues. She also talked to two students who identified as gay or lesbian. Each of these students (unknown to each other) had talked to their parents about their identities, and each one had been met with hostility. Rowland knew that these students were hurting and that they needed extra support. One day, she told her secretary, Elaine Monell, that if either of these students needed to see her because of these issues, Monell should let them right in rather than require them to schedule an appointment.[8]

In Rowland's memory decades later, Monell then peppered her with questions, including whether Rowland had disclosed her own sexual identity to these students. Rowland said that the students had asked her if she too was gay, and recognizing that they were looking for support, she answered honestly that she was bisexual. In Rowland's memory, Monell immediately went to her supervisor, who went to the principal, who called Rowland in to his office at the end of that day. Rowland "knew something was up, because there was a hush around the secretary's office, which was outside of my office, and every time I would go out to go to a classroom or the restroom, I was being followed. I was being monitored by some student messenger. I could tell I was being followed, but I didn't know what was happening."[9] What was happening was that the principal, Alex DiNino, did not want Rowland to continue as a counselor in the school. He sent a student messenger with a note requesting that she come to his office, which she did. He had heard that she had told students and staff about her sexuality and told her, "We can't have that; it's not compatible here, so I'm going to give you this opportunity to resign." She responded, "I won't do that."[10]

Official documents tell the story a little differently, but the essentials are the same. According to a petition to the U.S. Sixth Circuit Court of Appeals, the mother of one of the gay students had come to meet with Rowland. That meeting did not go well. Rowland encouraged the mother to accept the young person's sexuality, advice that was "met with open hostility and accusations."[11] After this meeting, Rowland went to speak with the assistant principal about the situation, and in the course of that meeting, she told him of her identity as a bisexual woman. The assistant principal went to the principal with this information, and the principal then called Rowland in for the meeting in which he asked her to resign.

Following that meeting in which she refused to resign, Rowland went back to her office. Shortly thereafter another student brought another message, telling her to meet at a district building at the end of the school day. Rowland guessed, correctly, that they were going to have her meet with the district superintendent, Raymond Hopper. Rather than go alone, she called a lawyer with the ACLU, whose advertisement she had seen, and he accompanied her to that meeting. That lawyer, Asher Bogin, quickly grasped the issue at stake and pushed Superintendent Hopper to articulate his position. "How," Bogin asked, "is being lesbian or bisexual any different from belonging to the Rotary Club?"[12] That is, her right to free association and free speech should be protected, so long as it did not interfere with the performance of her job. Hopper's response was to once again offer Rowland the opportunity to resign. "And at that time," Rowland remembers, "instead of just sitting still, I just stood up and I said, 'I will not resign.'" Hopper then suspended her effective immediately and told her, "You're not to go to your office, you're not to go over there [to the school], you're not to take anything out of your office, and you will hear from us."[13] Rowland had been hired under a one-year contract, and the district was legally required to honor that contract. They could not fire her, but they could suspend her, which they did. And they could opt not to renew her contract when the time for renewals came in the spring.

When Rowland had first signed on to work at Mad River School District, she joined the union, the National Education Association (NEA). She almost opted not to; although the dues were not high, this was her first job after completing her master's degree in counseling, she had little money, and she had three small children. It would have been easy not to join. But she did join, and it was to her union she now turned for help. Her timing was propitious. It was only that year—1974—when the NEA changed its policy to one that offered protection for gay and lesbian educators. This change was pivotal for Rowland, as for the next eleven years as her case wound its way through filings, trial, and appeals, all her legal representation was provided by the NEA. If Rowland had been fired by Mad River one year earlier, the union would not have paid for any of this, and it is likely that Rowland would not have been able to afford to defend herself in court.

One of the first things Rowland's NEA legal representation did was to file a suit for reinstatement. They did this in February 1975 and won. The judge ruled that because Rowland had not been given a hearing, she could not be discharged, suspended, or otherwise disciplined. When she reported for work, however, the district gave her nothing to do. Rowland then filed a contempt of court motion against the principal and superintendent for ignoring the judge's order.[14] Again she won. This time when she returned to work, the district "assigned her to a newly created position outside the high school building, permitted her no student contact, and instructed her to develop a career education curriculum."[15] Rowland had never been accused of inappropriate conduct with students. To bar her from any contact with students was to play into the notion of homosexuals as out-of-control sexual aggressors and pedophiles.

That spring, just weeks after the court ordered the district to give Rowland work to do, the board met to vote on contract renewals for the district. Rowland's principal and superintendent both recommended that her contract not be renewed, and the board followed their recommendation. On June 3, Rowland filed a lawsuit against the district.[16] For the next ten years, Rowland and her NEA-funded lawyers fought for her reinstatement as a counselor. In this lawsuit, they fought for nondiscrimination in employment on the basis of sexuality and for freedom of speech on the part of educators.

It took Rowland six years just to get a trial.

For the first several years, lawyers for the school district, the superintendent, and the principal—each of whom had been named in Rowland's lawsuit—argued that there was no case. Rowland's lawyers had argued that her Fourteenth Amendment rights to due process had been violated because her termination had been "arbitrary and capricious." This argument was tossed out in one summary judgment because she had been hired with a limited one-year contract, and therefore she had no reason to expect continued employment.[17] Her lawyers then argued that she had been fired because she had told others of her bisexuality. Carl B. Rubin, the judge hearing the school district's request for summary judgment, sided with the district, saying that there was no basis for Rowland's suit to go to trial. Rubin ruled that Rowland "had no legal redress after she made her sexual preferences known" and that the school district was "entitled to take her sexual preferences into consideration" in deciding not to renew her contract.[18] The use of summary judgment as a way to avoid trial is "particularly dangerous to the party against whom the motion is made," as it uses technicalities to prevent a trial from happening.[19] For two years, one basis after another for the suit was dismissed by Judge Rubin. Notwithstanding all these setbacks, Rowland kept appealing for a full hearing. Then, in August 1977, Rubin made a pronouncement: Rowland's case had no merit because sexual orientation was not a constitutionally protected class; therefore, she could not make a case for equal protection.[20]

Rowland remembered Judge Rubin as being "really homophobic."[21] Others in the Dayton area might remember Rubin for his involvement in those same years in a school busing case. Rubin had been appointed to the bench by President Richard M. Nixon in 1971. Not long after that, he presided over a desegregation case in Dayton. Initially agreeing that the district was engaged in racial segregation, he later apparently changed his mind. Just months after his final ruling against Rowland, Rubin "voided a busing program," saying that "evidence of intent to segregate had not been provided by the National Association for the Advancement of Colored People."[22] In both the busing case and in the Rowland case, Rubin took politically conservative stances. His decision against Rowland in August 1977 was a major blow. It would be another two and a half years before that decision was overturned.

For that to happen, Rowland needed to get her position heard by someone other than Rubin. Rowland took her case to the U.S. Sixth Circuit Court of Appeals, where it was heard by a three-judge panel. Finally, in January 1980, these judges sent the case back to district court for a trial. Rowland remembers one of those judges saying, "It is time for this woman to have her day in court."[23] That day would actually last twenty-three days, and it would take close to two years before it would begin.[24]

From the time her contract was not renewed in the spring of 1975 until the trial finally began in the fall of 1981, Rowland kept busy. She was involved in all the legal filings and hearings, of course, which took up a lot of time and a lot of mental and emotional energy. Her primary concern, though, was supporting her three children as a single parent. She had just earned her master's degree in counseling right before being hired by Mad River, and she loved working in a school setting. But she knew there "was no point" in applying for jobs in nearby school districts, as Mad River officials had threatened her that if she refused to resign, she would be "blacklisted."[25] She did, though, apply to substitute teach in Yellow Springs, the more liberal community where she lived. To her shock, that district, too, turned her away. Once again, her attorneys "went to bat" for her, and she was able to be a substitute teacher there.[26] Clearly this was not going to be a good long-term solution, and anyway, she wanted to work as a counselor.

For the next several years, Rowland worked for social service agencies in the area. She became a supervisor of outpatient youth in a drug program in Dayton for a year and then went to work for the Mental Health Association of Greene County, in the nearby town of Xenia, Ohio. There she gave workshops on stress reduction, a topic in which she surely had great personal experience. Somewhere along the line, she began doing volunteer work at a local domestic violence shelter. "While I was doing that," she later recalled, "being an advocate for women, it occurred to me it would be really a good idea if I could go to court with them and really do something."[27] In 1978 she entered law school, graduating in 1981—just months before her own case finally went to trial. When she was raising three small children, going to law school, doing volunteer work, and trying to keep her own case moving forward, she barely earned enough money to support her household. During some of those years, she received governmental aid in the form of food stamps. Receiving those stamps would later come back to haunt her.

Rowland engaged in other forms of volunteer work, as well, during those years between her contract nonrenewal and her trial. In 1975 she was a member of the Yellow Springs Human Rights Commission when the village passed a nondiscrimination law protecting the civil rights of homosexuals and bisexuals. That such a law passed was unusual. East Lansing, Michigan, was the first municipality to ban discrimination based on sexual orientation, which it did in 1972.[28] Washington, DC, followed in 1973, while New York City rejected a similar ordinance that same year. Even San Francisco, thought always to be a frontrunner in gay rights, did not ban discrimination based on sexual orientation until 1978.[29] So although there was some precedent, the cities that established these protections were few and far between in 1975.

Not only was Yellow Springs among the first municipalities to protect LGBT rights; it did so in an unusual way. Rather than write a new law that banned discrimination against homosexuals, as East Lansing and Washington had, the Yellow Springs council amended its law banning sex discrimination by broadening its definition of "sex" to include "sexual orientation and manifestations."[30] Federal courts would not similarly broaden the definition of sex in this way until the Seventh Circuit Court of Appeals ruled on the *Hively v. Ivy Tech* case in April 2017. Then, for the first time, a federal court ruled that discrimination based on sexual orientation can be litigated as a case of sex discrimination under Title VII of the Civil Rights Act of 1964, which bans discrimination in employment on the basis of sex.[31] This reasoning provided the fulcrum of the 2020 *Bostock v. Clayton County* decision.

In 1977, Dade County, Florida, passed a gay rights ordinance, which was quickly and viciously fought by the fundamentalist entertainer Anita Bryant and her Save Our Children campaign. As discussed in chapter 1, Bryant started a massive crusade to force a referendum on the issue, and turnout was high. That summer, voters turned out two-to-one to repeal the law, and

Bryant went on to fight against civil rights for gays and lesbians across the country. In particular, she stoked the flames of people's fears that children needed to be protected from gays and lesbians, inside and outside the classroom.[32]

The frenzy of Bryant's Dade County efforts culminated in passing the referendum in June 1977. In July, a story went out on the Associated Press wire about Yellow Springs's "very unusual" approach to gay rights. Interviewed for that story was Marjorie Rowland, who had been a member of the human rights commission two years before when Yellow Springs redefined sex to include sexual orientation. Rowland's final court hearing with Judge Rubin was the following month, August 1977. This was the hearing in which his dismissal of her case led to the case being moribund for another two and a half years, until it was heard by the three-judge panel in an appeals court. It is impossible to know how much impact the Florida events had on Rowland's hearing that summer. Certainly, Judge Rubin had already ruled against her in previous summary judgments. But Anita Bryant's Save Our Children campaign in Florida stirred the pot of public sentiment on an unprecedented scale. And then to have the Yellow Springs law garner national attention, and for none other than Marjorie Rowland herself to be highlighted as being involved in the creation of that law, and for all of this to happen just weeks before what would be the final summary judgment hearing on the Mad River case, surely had some impact.

In the article about the Yellow Springs law that went out over the national wire, Rowland referred to other "problems [that] have come up." She noted a discrimination complaint lodged against the local newspaper, the *Yellow Springs News*; the complaint led to an apology from the newspaper to the Antioch–Yellow Springs Gay Center. She also said—and the newspaper reporter did not follow up on this—that she believed that "an avowed homosexual would have trouble getting a teaching or counseling job in Yellow Springs."[33] She knew this firsthand, of course, having applied for a job in that district in 1975 and being turned away. Only after her lawyers intervened was she allowed to work as a substitute teacher. By 1977 Rowland had no reason to believe that the situation had changed. The reporter apparently did not know that Rowland was involved in a lawsuit regarding this very issue in a neighboring city.

The article also mentioned that in 1976 when the Human Rights Commission sponsored a Gay Awareness Weekend, the town council was inundated with calls from taxpayers who opposed council funding of the

FIG. 2.1 Marjorie Rowland at the time of the *Rowland v. Mad River* case

weekend. The Commission had to fund it with private donations, and even at that, townspeople protested. In spite of all these examples of "problems," the article quoted Rowland as saying that "homosexual rights . . . [is] not a burning issue" in Yellow Springs and that no one had filed any complaints of job or housing discrimination.[34] Decades later, Rowland remembered Yellow Springs as "a very supportive community." When asked what part of the community was supportive, she said, "All of them, really."[35] Given that she had not been allowed to teach there initially, that she believed no "avowed homosexual" would be allowed to teach, that the town council did not help fund a gay awareness activity, and that the event had protesters even when it had been privately funded, it is difficult from this vantage point to see the entire community as supportive. Were there enough sympathetic or like-minded people that even if their numbers were small, their significance was enormous in a world that otherwise felt utterly hostile? Or were the antigay voices loud but few in number? Clearly Rowland experienced Yellow Springs as a safe and liberal haven during her years there. At the least, this is a reminder that even communities that see themselves—and are seen by others—as liberal can be selectively liberal and can still exhibit discriminatory biases at times. Yellow Springs was liberal enough to pass an unusual nondiscrimination statute, but not so liberal that its school board didn't turn away an experienced educator who was "an avowed" bisexual. The village was liberal enough to hold a Gay Awareness Week, but not liberal enough to fund it. Demarcations of liberalism are not clear cut, are deeply contextual, often are in the eye of the beholder, and change greatly even in the space of a few years.

By fall of 1981 when her case finally went to trial, Rowland had become an attorney and an activist. She had earned her law degree and passed the Ohio bar in May 1981. She had helped her town of Yellow Springs to craft a new civil rights law that would garner national attention for its distinctiveness. And now she was pursuing social justice by arguing for rights for homosexual teachers.

The Trial

The case was multifaceted, involving three separate actions on the part of the school district, three causes for the actions, and various district administrators. The three actions were Rowland's suspension, her being transferred to a new position that did not involve student conduct, and the nonrenewal of her contract. The three causes on which the jury had to deliberate were Rowland's bisexuality, Rowland's disclosing her bisexuality to others in the school, and her having filed a lawsuit against the district after her suspension and after the transfer before her contract was not renewed.

Three constitutional rights were at issue: the right of access to the courts, the right of equal protection of the law, and the right of free speech.

Everyone in the case agreed that the Constitution did not grant anyone the right to be homosexual or bisexual. But the other constitutional rights existed regardless of Rowland's sexual identity. Had those rights been violated? Had the district retaliated for Rowland's lawsuits against them when they opted not to renew her contract? Had the district violated her right to equal protection by treating her differently than other employees simply because she was bisexual? Had they violated her right to free speech when they fired her for telling people of her sexual identity? These were the key questions of the case.

Rowland and her lawyers argued that the district had infringed on her rights. The lawyers for the principal, superintendent, and school board made different arguments. They said that Rowland had not been suspended, transferred, or let go because of her sexuality but because she was not good at her job. They contended that she "was a 'free spirit' who had embarked on an 'uncharted course' and was operating in an unconventional manner" and therefore was not fit to be a guidance counselor.[36] District officials pointed to two incidents as examples of her behaving badly in her role as guidance counselor. The first incident involved the two students who identified as gay and who were having trouble at home because of their sexuality. When Rowland gave their names to her secretary, Monell, she violated their confidentiality, the district said. Expert witnesses testified that it would indeed be an ethics violation for a counselor to disclose these students' names and their sexuality unless there was a compelling reason in the students' interest to do so, or unless the students had said it was acceptable to them. The district argued that it was not necessary to reveal their names, and she should not have done so. Rowland said that it *was* necessary, because Monell was not sympathetic to these students' need to see Rowland and was in fact making it difficult for the students. Rowland told Monell about their trouble at home to make clear to Monell that she should let them in to see her. Rowland also said that the students had given her permission to disclose their names and sexual identity if she felt she needed to.[37]

The second incident occurred when Rowland had been asked to take over an English class for a particular session. The district claimed that Rowland asked the class inappropriate questions about their personal lives, sexual habits, and sexual orientations, that she told the class about her own sexual identity, and that she talked to them about sex with her girlfriend. Rowland said instead that her role in the class was to read and respond to questions that the class submitted and to facilitate class discussion and that most of the students' questions were about sex.[38]

Whose accounts were true? To get at the specifics of these issues, the judge used "special verdict forms." Special verdicts are used in courtrooms when the judge wants the jury to make decisions about disputed facts of the case rather than decide guilt or liability. The judge then renders the verdict based on those answers.[39] In this case, the jury received forms that included fifty-six special verdict questions. They had to determine not only what had happened but exactly who (principal, superintendent, school board) had done what.

The first set of special verdict questions revolved around Rowland's having told her secretary, Elaine Monell, that she was in love with a woman. Jurors first were asked whether Rowland's statement "in any way interfere[d] with the proper performance" of either Rowland's or Monell's duties or with the regular operation of the school? Then they were asked whether the principal's and superintendent's series of decisions—first to suspend Rowland, then to transfer her, and finally to not renew her contract—were motivated at least in part by Rowland's statement to Monell about her sexuality. The jury answered that Rowland's statement in no way interfered with anyone's ability to do their job or to keep the school running smoothly, and the jury answered that yes, each of the actions by each of the administrators was indeed motivated by Rowland's statement.[40]

The second set of special verdict questions centered on the student who identified as a lesbian and whose mother had been upset by Rowland's advice to accept her daughter. Following that encounter, Rowland had been concerned enough that she went to the assistant principal, Thomas Goheen, to discuss it, saying that she was worried about her job. He told her that "she should not be concerned and that he would keep the matter confidential." The jury was asked the same set of questions about Rowland's statement to the assistant principal as they were asked about her statement to Monell. Once again, the jury answered that Rowland's statement in no way interfered with anyone's ability to do their job, and that yes, the administrators' decisions were motivated at least in part by her statement to the assistant principal.

The third set of special verdict questions repeated the same questions, only this time regarding her statements to fellow teachers about her sexuality. Once again, the jury found that her statements did not keep anyone from doing their job, and that yes, these statements were part of the motivation for the administrators' actions.

The first three sets of special verdicts were a victory for Rowland. They established clearly that her statements had not disrupted the school in any way and that the jury believed that her being suspended, transferred, and ultimately let go were because of the administration's views regarding her sexuality.

The fourth set of questions asked about whether the administration had retaliated against Rowland for filing her first lawsuits. Had they transferred her to a position not involving students, and had they not renewed her contract, in part because she had filed lawsuits? In all these eight questions, the jury sided with the district and felt that retaliation had not been a factor in any of their decisions.

The fifth set of questions asked whether Rowland was treated differently because of her sexuality. Here, the jury found that the principal and superintendent had treated her differently than other employees simply because of her sexuality. But the jury drew the line when it came to the board of education, finding that they had not treated her any differently. This was because the board generally followed the recommendation of the superintendent and did so in this case, as well. This was made clear in a different set of special verdicts (the seventh set), in which the jury found that the board followed its usual procedure.

The sixth set of questions went to the question of intent. The jury was asked to consider whether the administration had acted in good faith: "sincerely and with a belief that he is doing right, and his conduct is justified by an objectively reasonable belief that it was lawful."[41] Or, on the other hand, were the officials maliciously trying to deprive Rowland of her constitutional rights? The jury was convinced that all the administrative officials had acted in good faith at each step.

The final set of questions asked whether the jury believed that Rowland would have been suspended, transferred, and had her contract not renewed if she had never told anyone of her sexuality. The jury answered no, in all cases. All the actions against her occurred not based on job performance but on her statements regarding her sexuality.

The jury, then, answered some of the major questions of the case: No, the district had not retaliated against Rowland when they opted not to renew her contract. Yes, the district—in the offices of principal and superintendent—had violated her right to equal protection by treating her differently than other employees simply because she was bisexual, but the school board had not. Yes, the principal and superintendent—but again, not the school board—had infringed on her right to free speech when they fired her for telling people of her sexual identity.

The trial was not over after the jury reached its special verdicts, because now the judge had to make his decision. Lawyers for each side once again had an opportunity to make arguments. Here they addressed the issue of free speech. During the trial, lawyers for the district argued that Rowland had not been let go because of what she said about being bisexual but because of her poor job performance. Now they argued that even if the district had let her go because of what she had revealed, that would not have been protected speech, anyway. The right to free speech is not an absolute right; people cannot just say anything they want at any time. Earlier cases, especially the *Pickering* case in 1968, had established the need to strike "a balance between the interests of the teacher, as a citizen, in connecting upon matters of public concern and the interest of the State, as an employer, in promoting the efficiency of the public services it performs through its employees."[42] During the trial, the district's lawyers had argued that her speech had disrupted the "efficiency" of the school. The jury, though, found otherwise, concluding that Rowland's speech had not interfered at all in the work of the school, and therefore her speech should be protected.

Now the district's lawyers argued instead that her speech was not protected because it was about a private matter; she was not speaking on a "matter of public concern." Judge Robert A. Steinberg disagreed, writing in his opinion that an educator has the right "to express her innermost personal thoughts, her doubts, her fears, her insecurities, her likes, and her loves to fellow workers and friends so long as she does not impede the performance of the public school function."[43] Even though the jury's special verdicts had determined that the school board merely followed the recommendation of the superintendent in not renewing Rowland's contract, the judge found differently. Judge Steinberg argued that the board knew full well that the superintendent's recommendation was based on Rowland's disclosure about her sexuality; given that in Steinberg's view this disclosure was protected speech, this then was "constitutionally impermissible reasoning" for her being fired.[44] He therefore held the board liable. This very important issue of defining the limits of free speech for public school teachers would be addressed again in the appeals that followed the trial.

In his opinion, Judge Steinberg addressed the district's contention that Rowland had been fired because of her unconventional approach. He wrote that "a person has the constitutional right to be different" and that in our public educational system, "which should have as one of its highest values the free expression of thoughts and ideas, there is room for the 'free spirit,' the unconventional person who marches to the beat of 'a different drummer.'"[45] The jury was dismissed after the judge rendered his verdict and had to reconvene a few weeks later to determine the amount of compensation Rowland would be awarded. The Dayton area included people who were not at all inclined to allow for different drummers. The judge received calls from irate parents, one of whom expressed an intention to appear in court during this next phase of the proceedings wearing an armband in protest. Radio talk shows and a newspaper account expressed concern that this case would "bankrupt the school system." Rowland reported having

FIG. 2.2 Marjorie Rowland

gotten obscene calls after one such radio show. Judge Steinberg requested that Federal Protective Officers be present in case protesters harassed Rowland, the lawyers, or the jury. The jury awarded Rowland $40,447 in compensation for lost income and damages.[46]

The trial was a victory for Rowland and potentially for any professionally responsible "free spirit" in the public schools.

Rowland could not celebrate, though. In fact, she was immediately forced into temporary hiding.

New Problems

The jury had delivered each of its fifty-six special verdicts, one by one. The process took most of the afternoon. "Each time they read one and you're holding your breath," until "after a while, you've got enough of the picture that it's going to be a good thing," Rowland recalled.[47] Rowland and her team could see that the jury had seen the issues in the way that favored Rowland. The judge then dismissed the jury, and Rowland was waiting for his decision. In that space of time—excited, hopeful, on the brink of feeling happy and relieved that she might have won her case—that was when a reporter approached her in the courtroom and asked, "Ms. Rowland, what is your reaction to the secret indictment?"[48] Rowland had no idea about an indictment, secret or otherwise. Her attorney told her, "Do not go home. They are going to arrest you." Rowland and her partner and their children went to a hotel where they hid out for several days until her lawyers got a handle on what was going on.[49]

On Friday, October 24, 1981, Marjorie Rowland was indicted on food stamp fraud: two counts of theft by deception and two counts of falsifying the number of dependents on food stamp applications.[50] She allegedly received food stamp overpayments totaling about $1,000 between September 1979 and June 1980.[51] For this, she faced a maximum of five years in prison and a $2,500 fine for the felony charges and a maximum of six months in prison and a $1,000 fine for the misdemeanor charges.[52]

The fact is, she was guilty. She did receive overpayments. Rowland received food stamps during the years that she was a law student. Although she had custody of all three of her children, and all three lived with her when she applied for the food stamps, the oldest child sometimes opted to stay with her father. Later, another child "began a series of moves" between her two parents' homes, while "deciding which parent to live with."[53] As a result, some of the time during those months Rowland received food stamps for children who were living with their father rather than with her.

At least two things stand out about the food stamp charges. First, the timing is interesting, to say the least. The indictments were voted on precisely during the weeks of her trial, which was a very public case.[54] Assistant Prosecutor Gregory Lockhart said the timing was "coincidental" and that "irregularities in Rowland's food stamp applications first came to light during a random check of food stamp applicants."[55] That led to an investigation and the eventual charges. It may have indeed been coincidental timing, but it would have been quite a coincidence.

Second, how Rowland's fraud case was handled was different from how other similar cases were handled. Rowland's lawyer investigated and found that the Greene County prosecutor's office had a history of bargaining welfare fraud cases whenever some effort toward restitution was made by the person charged with fraud. In other words, if a welfare recipient made good on the overpayment, charges might be reduced from felonies to misdemeanors or be dropped altogether.[56] When Rowland first became aware of the overpayment, she "wrote them a letter and apologized. I explained the situation and offered to make restitution. This is why I'm absolutely shocked that criminal charges have been filed," she said in an interview at the time.[57] In her case, the prosecutor refused to plea bargain, and refused to accept her repayment. Refusing to plea bargain had the biggest potential implications for Rowland. If convicted of the felony charges, she would no longer be able to practice law in the state.

The prosecutor in Greene County was a man named William F. Schenck. Schenck was known for his "dogged determination to get the job done, no matter how unconventional the means."[58] Schenck was a colleague and close friend of Mike DeWine, a former county prosecutor who went on to become a Republican member of the Ohio State Senate, the U.S. House of Representatives, U.S. Senate, lieutenant governor of Ohio, attorney general of Ohio, and Ohio governor. DeWine said about Schenck that "tough cases ended up in convictions that would not have been pursued by most prosecutors."[59] Several years after the Rowland case, Schenck was charged with prosecutorial misconduct in his handling of another case. Attorney Barry Wilford said about Schenck that he "is one of those guys who's too small to kick and too wet to step on. In other words, we don't trust him."[60]

Schenck opted not to prosecute the fraud case against Rowland himself, saying that "justice would be better served if we could get someone to take an objective look at this case without any ties to the Greene County Welfare Department or the legal community."[61] Why did he feel he could not be objective in this case? He said it was simply because Rowland was a lawyer in the county and that he and his office might need to work with her in the future. Rowland, however, believed that Schenck had an issue with her sexuality. When she had become a lawyer, he signed her application to practice in the county—a formality. He had no reason then to know about her sexuality or about her then-forthcoming case against Mad River School District. She believes that when he found out, he became either embarrassed or angry that he had given his signature to her application to practice law.[62]

Schenck contacted Craig Albert, who had been assistant prosecutor in Greene County before becoming prosecutor in Geauga County, Ohio. Albert had a reputation there for being "outspoken" and "controversial."[63] In 1981, he had just arrived in Geauga County; he would remain there for thirty-six years, first as prosecutor, then as municipal court judge, and then as county commissioner. As judge, he received national attention when he suggested that someone needed a green card to drive through his county. As commissioner, he again got national notice when he suggested requiring welfare recipients to be sterilized.[64] This is the person Schenck thought could be more objective than him on Rowland's case.

Timeline of Events in Rowland's Case

May 1975	Contract not renewed
January–June 1977	Anita Bryant's Save Our Children campaign in Florida
August 1977	Case dismissed by Judge Rubin
January 1980	Appeals court demands a trial
October 1981	District court trial; Rowland wins
October 1981	Rowland indicted for food stamp fraud
March 1984	Appeals court overturns trial verdict; Rowland loses
February 1985	U.S. Supreme Court refuses to hear Rowland's case
April 1985	Rehearing denied by U.S. Supreme Court
December 1985	Food stamp fraud case settled
1986	Moves to Arizona; denied admission to the bar
1992	Admitted to Arizona bar

In the end, Rowland's lawyers managed to achieve a plea bargain in the fraud case, but largely only because Rowland filed suit in federal court. This, too, took years. Although the indictment was filed in October 1981, the case was not settled until December 1985. At that point, she pled guilty to one count of misdemeanor in exchange for the prosecutor dropping all the remaining charges and Rowland dropping her lawsuit against them. She got a suspended thirty-day jail sentence and a $250 fine.[65]

Before the food stamp fraud case was over, however, Rowland had to go through several rounds of appeals on her Mad River case.

The Appeals

Rowland's lawsuit against Mad River School District ended successfully in October 1981, when the jury made clear that she had been suspended, transferred, and had her contract not renewed because she told people in the school about her sexuality. Judge Steinberg had found the principal, superintendent, and the school board liable and awarded Rowland payment for lost wages. She did not get those lost wages, though, as the school district quickly filed an appeal. That appeal was heard in the U.S. Sixth Circuit Court of Appeals in March 1984—nearly a full decade after she had been fired. As an appeals case, there was no jury; the case was decided by a panel of three judges.

The chief circuit judge was Frederick Pierce Lively, who was born in Louisville, Kentucky, served in the U.S. Navy during World War II, and attended law school at the University of Virginia. He was appointed to the bench by President Nixon in 1972. He was a strong advocate of separation of church and state and was remembered as someone who embodied "gentleness and civility."[66]

Also on the panel was Robert Krupansky from Cleveland, Ohio, who had served in the U.S. Army Air Corps during World War II and studied law at Case Western Reserve University. Krupansky had been appointed to the district court by President Nixon and to the circuit court of appeals by President Ronald Reagan. Lawyers reputedly referred to Judge Krupansky as "Whispering Death," as someone with a "penchant for using a five-dollar word when a 50-cent word would suffice," and who had "firm (to put it mildly) control of his courtroom."[67] One scholar wrote that Krupansky "seemingly never saw a civil rights case he could uphold."[68] The conservative writer Russell Kirk once wrote that procedural reforms were needed "to restrain the tortuous ingenuity of judges like Robert Krupansky."[69]

Finally, the appeals panel included George Clifton Edwards Jr. Edwards had been appointed to the bench by President John F. Kennedy in September 1963 and was confirmed shortly after Kennedy's assassination. Born in Texas, he moved to Detroit, Michigan, in the midst of the Depression and worked as a union organizer. He too had served in the army during World War II. After the war, he earned his law degree from Detroit College of Law. He ran for mayor of Detroit in 1949 but lost "in a racially charged election in which Edwards stood up for equal rights for blacks and the protection of individual civil rights." His father also had been a lawyer and an "activist on behalf of labor unions, the poor, and African Americans."[70] The very year that Rowland had been fired and filed her first lawsuit, Edwards published a biography of his father. The book begins with the son's confirmation hearing before the Senate Judiciary Committee, "when the senators were prepared to pardon him for his father's radical sins—but the son feels no need for such absolution."[71] Not surprisingly given his background, he was the only one out of the three judges who took seriously the constitutional threats embedded in Rowland's case.

When the Mad River School District appealed Rowland's victory in the lower court, it argued that neither Rowland's First Amendment right to freedom of speech nor her Fourteenth Amendment right to equal protection of the law had been violated. The majority of the appeals court judges agreed with this position. They agreed with the district's argument that Rowland's speech was not protected because her disclosure of her sexuality was a personal matter, not a matter of public concern. As evidence they noted that Rowland had told her secretary, Monell, in confidence of her relationship with another woman and that when she went to the assistant principal with her concern about the angry parent, she asked him, too, to keep her revelation confidential. "Thus," the judges argued in their published opinion, her "own treatment of the issue of her sexual preference indicates that she recognized that the matter was not one of public concern."[72] As a private matter, it was not protected speech, and the First Amendment did not apply.

The equal protection claim was more complicated. First, the board had both permissible and nonpermissible reasons for not renewing Rowland's contract, and the special verdicts had not clarified which reasons were the actual reasons behind the decision. In the special verdicts, the judge had combined the fact of Rowland's bisexuality with her talking about her bisexuality and had not included Rowland's disclosing confidential information about the students to her secretary. The jury had been asked, "If she had not been bisexual, *and* if she had not told others," would she have been fired? The jury answered no. But the jury was not asked if she had been fired solely because of her bisexuality *or* whether talking about her sexuality was the reason for her dismissal. Nor had they been asked if disclosing information about the students might have been reasonable cause for dismissal, regardless of either her sexuality or her speech about herself. In giving out that confidential information about her students, had she failed in her duty? To prove that she had been discriminated against, she needed to prove that she had done her job well and was fired only because of the discrimination. Two of the three appeals court judges concluded that in fact she had *not* done her job well, because she had unnecessarily violated students' confidentiality.

Second, the judges argued that there was no way to know if Rowland had been treated differently on the basis of her sexuality, because there was no basis for comparison. Jurors had been asked in those special verdicts about "similarly situated" employees, but there were no similarly situated employees. No other school employees were found to have violated students' confidentiality or to have talked in similar ways about their sexuality. As Judge Lively put it, no heterosexual employees made "their personal sexual preferences the topic of comment and discussion in the high school community."[73] Therefore, it was impossible to know if Rowland was treated differently. The majority decision, then, was to reverse the lower court decision.

Judge Edwards, the man who had worked for unions during the Depression and who had lost a mayoral run because of his advocacy for African

Americans, disagreed with the majority decision. While earlier judges had dismissed Rowland's case in summary judgments because there was no constitutional protection based on sexuality, Edwards wrote, "I find no language in the Constitution of the United States which excludes citizens who are bisexual or homosexual from its protection."[74] Instead, he said, homosexuals are protected, too, "certainly to the extent of being homosexual and stating their sexual preference in a factual manner where there is no invasion of any other person's rights."[75] Edwards disagreed with the other two judges on both of the major constitutional issues at stake.

Regarding the First Amendment, Edwards wrote in his dissenting opinion that Rowland's bisexuality was indeed a public, not merely a private, concern. The issue of homosexual rights "has swirled nationwide for many years," and the fact that she talked to the assistant principal about her sexuality "in an effort to establish her right to her job while admitting being bisexual" is evidence of the link of her speech to that broader public issue.[76] Edwards further alluded to "organized parental pressure" on the school to boot Rowland out of her job, and that in itself was evidence that Rowland was in the middle of "a controversy in process over an important public issue."[77] He concluded, then, that her speech was protected under the First Amendment and that her right to that speech had been violated.

Regarding the Fourteenth Amendment, Edwards made an analogy about race. Suppose Rowland was someone who could "pass" for white but had an African American parent. Suppose further that there were community protests when people found out, and those protests pressured the principal and school board to fire her. In that case, there would not be any doubt that her rights were violated. "I find no logical equal protection distinction between these two minority discrimination situations," Edwards wrote.[78]

Edwards dismissed the notion that there was no evidence that Rowland had been treated differently, as his colleague had written in the majority opinion. The jury had heard "ample evidence," Edwards wrote, that she would not have been suspended, transferred, or let go if she had not been bisexual. The jury "clearly did not believe that the above actions would have been taken against Rowland" if she were heterosexual.[79] Her naming the two students and disclosing their sexuality in confidence to her secretary, as a means of ensuring that the students got the help they needed, would not have led to that sequence of disciplinary actions if a straight counselor had done them.

Edwards then, in an eloquent closing, directly challenged the majority opinion as written by Lively. "My colleague's opinion," he wrote, treats this case "as if it involved only a single person and a sick one at that—in short, that plaintiff's admission of homosexual status was sufficient in itself to justify her termination."[80] Instead, he stated, homosexuality is not a mental disease, and Rowland was not alone. He cited the *Diagnostic and Statistical Manual II (DSMII) of Mental Disorders* of the American Psychiatric Association, which in 1974 had removed homosexuality as a type of mental disorder. He also cited the Kinsey studies and other works that documented the prevalence of homosexuality. "This school teacher has been deprived of her job solely because she let it be known to some colleagues, and through them, to her administrative superiors that her sexual preference was for another woman," Edwards wrote.[81] Clearly, he felt that this was wrong and that the lower court, which had found for Rowland, was right. But he was one of only three judges in the appeals court to take this stand, and so the lower court decision was overturned. Rowland had lost.

Rowland may have lost that round, but she had not given up. The next strategy was to request a *rehearing en banc*. The appeals case that she lost had been heard by a three-member panel of circuit court judges. An en banc hearing meant that her case would be heard by all of the judges for the Sixth Circuit. Generally, en banc hearings only happen when a decision has been made that seems to contradict U.S. Supreme Court decisions. Rowland's attorneys argued that the decision in her case did contradict the Supreme Court. Her attorneys also argued that her case involved "questions of exceptional importance": whether freedom of speech applies to statements regarding sexual orientation and whether equal protection applies to being fired because of sexual orientation.[82] In other words, once again her attorneys were contending that Rowland's First and Fourteenth Amendment rights had been violated.

The request for the rehearing said that the appeals court had relied too heavily on Rowland having first spoken privately or confidentially to others about her sexuality. That court had said that those private utterances meant that the First Amendment right to free speech did not apply, because her speech was merely a personal concern. Rowland's lawyer now pointed out that yes, she had revealed her orientation to the assistant principal because she feared for her job, but that did not relegate it to a mere personal concern. She feared for her job precisely because her orientation was a public issue. Her lawyer used Judge Edwards's dissent as part of the argument, quoting his opinion where it said that "the same issue of homosexual rights which has swirled nationwide for many years" was the same issue that Rowland's speech reflected.[83] Furthermore, they argued, the school administrators asked Rowland to resign immediately when they learned of her orientation because they "believed that the community would be offended by a bisexual guidance counselor. They *feared* public reaction. Thus, the matters concerning Ms. Rowland's suspension and nonrenewal were matters of public concern and controversy."[84] In fact, they argued, Rowland's statements "were aimed at legal and social change which are at the core of First Amendment protections."[85]

The request for the rehearing once again used Judge Edwards's dissent as part of the argument on the equal protection clause. "There is no distinction," the request read, "between treating one differently due to racial considerations or considerations of sexual orientation."[86] The majority decision in the appeals case had argued that there was no evidence of "similarly situated" employees being treated differently. But Rowland's attorneys argued that they didn't need a comparison when they had direct statements from school officials saying that her orientation was central to the disciplinary actions taken against her. Beyond that, heterosexual employees routinely "display evidence of their sexual orientation such as pictures or wedding rings without suffering the same type of treatment" that Rowland received.[87] She was treated differently because of her orientation.

Requests for en banc hearings must show that the earlier judgment contradicts U.S. Supreme Court decisions. Here, Rowland's lawyers documented cases in which courts had made clear that dismissing an employee because of their sexual orientation was only allowable if there was clear evidence that the person's orientation directly affected their job performance. Then they demonstrated that nothing in Rowland's record showed that her orientation impaired the performance of her duties. Instead, trial testimony showed that teachers, students, and parents all believed that she was a good guidance counselor, and not a single teacher testified "that he or she would hesitate to refer any student to [Rowland] because of her sexual orientation."[88]

In spite of the rigor of these arguments, the request for a rehearing of the full circuit court was denied. Still, Rowland continued to fight. The only place to take her case now was to the U.S. Supreme Court. As we know from chapter 1, in February 1985 the Supreme Court declined to hear her case. Yet the fiery dissent written by Brennan helped to advance civil rights for LGBTQ people.

The Aftermath

By the time the news of the Supreme Court's decision came out, Rowland had been a practicing attorney in Yellow Springs for several years. The same month that Rowland's trial victory was overturned by the circuit court, she took on a case in which she represented another woman who had been fired from her job. This would have been a tough case to win. Claudette Roundtree had been on the Dayton police force for eight years when she was arrested in April 1983 for a series of actions: driving while intoxicated, carrying a weapon while intoxicated, and possession of marijuana. She was convicted on all three counts and did not dispute the marijuana charge, but Roundtree appealed the other two convictions. In March 1984 she was fired "for conduct unbecoming an officer and disgraceful conduct." Rowland set out to defend Roundtree, arguing that the dismissal was "premature" since Roundtree's appeals had not been decided yet.[89] In March 1986 Roundtree was again found guilty of driving while intoxicated, fined $500, and sentenced to 10 days in jail and a 120-day driver's license suspension.[90] Why Rowland took on this case is not clear, but it is easy to imagine that she commiserated with anyone who might have been fired unfairly. Attending to due process certainly was central to Rowland's own case.

Rowland's activism and political work continued. In June she became a member of the board for the West Central Chapter of the American Civil Liberties Union (ACLU).[91] That spring and summer, she became politically engaged in a topic that had been significant in her life since her volunteer work at the domestic violence shelter. She wrote and "lobbied vigorously" for a city ordinance that would require officers to make arrests in cases of domestic violence.[92] The ordinance was proposed at the town council meeting in March, where Rowland said that "three times in the past two months she received calls from women who were in battering situations where the police did not make an arrest but instead tried to talk with the offender."[93] In July, again speaking on behalf of the ordinance, Rowland claimed that in 1984 and 1985, Yellow Springs police "discouraged seven women, who were repeatedly beaten by their spouses, from pressing charges, and twice refused to press charges for women who insisted on legal action." All seven women were clients of Rowland's, and she said they had been beaten on average three to four times, yet police discouraged them from filing charges. Further, police outright "refused to file charges for two of the women who persisted." The women had to file the charges themselves.

The police chief, Rowland said, believes "that a man's home is his castle and (police) should only go in if it's murder." She said that police minimized the seriousness of the abuse by calling it "a lover's spat." Yellow Springs's police chief, James McKee, called Rowland a liar and denied her allegations.[94] In October, with the council still deliberating, Rowland was one of the speakers at a public forum debating the issue.[95] The ordinance never passed.

By the end of the year, Rowland was winding up her time in Ohio. Earlier she had filed paperwork to run for election as mayor of Yellow Springs, but by August she withdrew her candidacy.[96] In November she also withdrew from her board position with the ACLU.[97] That December was when she pleaded guilty to the reduced charges in the fraud charges against her, taking a misdemeanor plea to clear her record of felonies.[98] In 1986, she moved to Tucson, Arizona, where perhaps she thought she could leave all of this behind.

Rowland's parents had moved from Toledo, Ohio, to Tucson and now were aging and in need of help. Rowland decided to go. Arizona and Ohio did not have a reciprocity agreement regarding bar admission, and so Rowland would have to take the bar exam there to continue her practice. While studying for the exam and waiting to know the results, she again worked as a counselor, this time at an outpatient treatment center.[99] Counseling had always been a part of her professional identity, even while working as a lawyer.

Applicants to the bar in Arizona, as in many states, had to take an exam and had to pass muster with its Committee on Character and Fitness. Most of the questions on the long application were easy: citizenship, educational history, employment history, whether she had ever gotten in trouble at school, when and where she had previously practiced law, whether she had ever been accused of malpractice as a lawyer. But other questions led to trouble. "Have you ever been reprimanded, censured, suspended, disbarred, or otherwise disqualified" from any profession? "Were you ever discharged or have you ever resigned from any employment . . . after being told your conduct or work was unsatisfactory?" Of course, she had been suspended and let go from Mad River School District, and court records showed that she had been accused of both conduct and work that was unsatisfactory. "Have you ever been accused of or charged with fraud, perjury, misrepresentation, or false swearing in a judicial or administrative proceeding?" Rowland had been charged with fraud in the food stamp case. And, to keep from getting a felony charge, she had pleaded guilty to one count of misdemeanor fraud. "Have you been a party to any type of civil action (including divorce) in the past ten years?" Rowland had been in and out of court, going all the way up to the U.S.

Supreme Court, for the past ten years. The committee also asked for financial information, including whether the applicant had ever filed for bankruptcy.[100] At some point in the years after Rowland lost her school district job and before establishing her legal career, Rowland had filed for bankruptcy.[101]

The Committee on Character and Fitness turned Rowland's application down. She could not practice law in Arizona. The repercussions of standing up for her own and others' civil rights were far-reaching and long-lasting. She would try again, and, in the meantime, she continued to work as a counselor in the outpatient center, doing work that she enjoyed.

Rowland had committed no crimes. The school district had accused her of misconduct, but a jury had found that her conduct was acceptable and that the district had fired her because of their bias against gays, lesbians, and bisexuals. She had made an error in accepting food stamps but had tried to pay back the extra money and had been denied that opportunity, an opportunity that virtually all others in the same position were allowed. She was forced into pleading guilty to a lesser charge to get on with her life. And if, along the way, she had to declare bankruptcy, that was hardly a crime. In fact, one could argue that her pursuit of civil rights was exemplary. She was in the forefront of important First and Fourteenth Amendment cases, ones that several circuit court and U.S. Supreme Court judges were on the record as saying were crucial issues. Beyond that, she had worked for a decade or more on behalf of victims of domestic violence. Yet she was denied entrance to the Arizona bar. Two times she tried, and two times she was denied.

Finally, in 1992, someone told Rowland that the composition of the Committee on Character and Fitness had changed and that the new members were less conservative. "You're not going to have any problems now," she was told.[102] She applied once again, and this time she was admitted to the bar. She had had to wait six years. Rowland continues to work in both capacities, as lawyer and counselor, and relishes them both.

Rowland fought for an entire decade against what she saw as being unjustly fired from her job as a high school guidance counselor. She fought for her own civil rights and for the civil rights of all LGBTQ educators. Even though her first win in district court was overturned, her case had an impact on cases that followed. The dissents of Judge Edwards and especially Justice Brennan were used in subsequent cases to build a precedent for LGBTQ rights. In addition, Rowland's case would have an impact on freedom of speech cases over the next several decades. In the next chapter, we turn to the implications of her case.

3

The Meaning of *Mad River*

Implications of the Case

> Yet, while gay, lesbian, and bisexual
> citizens may have lost this battle, the
> war is not over. If we have learned
> anything as an evolving species, it is that
> no government, no religion, no institu-
> tion, and no political party can long
> oppress the inviolable dignity and spirit
> of human beings in their fight for
> fairness in the courts, access to justice,
> and equal protection of the laws.

In the 2004 edition of *Sexuality, Gender, and the Law*, William Eskridge and Nan Hunter note, "By outing Rowland, the state created her as an 'open bisexual' and as a political activist—and ultimately as a lawyer."[1] Indeed, the impact of Marjorie Rowland's court battles reached far beyond the compass of her own life. In this chapter we consider the influence that *Rowland v. Mad River* had on subsequent legal cases involving the military, marriage, and teaching.

Thirty-three distinct cases have cited *Rowland v. Mad River* as prece-dent.[2] Some of the earliest references to her case revolved around whether public officials could be held to account for violations of civil rights. In Rowland's case, the appeals court (the Sixth Circuit Court) decided that the principal, superintendent, and school board were not liable for any alleged damage done to Rowland (and, that court claimed, Rowland's civil rights had not been violated). The appeals court's argument was used in later cases. For example, in *Wagner v. Genesee County Board of Commissioners*, the court referenced *Rowland* to explain, "In order to impose liability on the local governmental units, a plaintiff would be required to identify the offending policy, show that the policy in fact caused the wrong alleged, and connect the policy to the government entity."[3] In other words, someone whose rights may have been violated would have to show that the school or business had a policy that explicitly infringed on someone's rights, connect the dots between that policy and any harm done to that person because of that policy, and show that the government (whether local, municipal, county, or state) had a hand in writing and enforcing that policy. In this way, *Rowland* was used to lay out a road map to pursue civil rights. It may have been a rocky and difficult road, but at least there was a more clearly defined path.

More pertinent to LGBT civil rights, other courts leveraged Justice Brennan's 1985 dissent in cases regarding free speech and equal protection claims. In many of these cases, judges acknowledged that gay men and lesbians fit into a special legal classification, citing Brennan's critical line from the *Rowland* dissent: "Homosexuals have historically been the object of pernicious and sustained hostility, and it is fair to say that discrimination against homosexuals is 'likely ... to reflect deep-seated prejudice rather than ... rationality.'"[4] Because of the history of hostility against lesbians and gay men, some judges have said that they fit into the legal category known as *quasi-suspect status*. This is important because if a group can be classified as *suspect* or *quasi-suspect*, then courts have to examine discriminatory laws and policies with a higher degree of scrutiny. Being in a suspect or quasi-suspect group means that there is reason for the courts to *suspect* that discrimination against them is because of long-standing bias against the group, and therefore the court should examine those laws or policies more carefully.

If government action encroaches on a protected liberty or fundamental right or involves people with a protected status, the courts submit the law to an examination that is known as *strict scrutiny*. In this case the government must show that the law in question meets a compelling state interest and is narrowly tailored to reduce the impact of any constitutional infringement. Most cases, however, fall at the other end of the legal spectrum. Under the *rational-basis standard*, the government need only show a legitimate interest in maintaining a law under review. Intermediate scrutiny allows courts to recognize categories of cases that fall between the end points of strict scrutiny and rational-basis review. Under intermediate scrutiny, the government would need to show that a law is substantially related to an important state interest.[5] Employment discrimination or marriage equality cases, for instance, might reach strict scrutiny analysis if a court agrees that a constitutional right is at stake or if it considers LGBT people as constituting a protected class. Justice Brennan plotted the course toward suspect classification in 1985, and, as the following analysis indicates, lower court decisions that followed *Rowland v. Mad River* often turned on this question.[6]

Although the U.S. Supreme Court did not rule on employment discrimination against LGBT workers until 2020, lower courts have addressed this issue multiple times. Five cases brought against the U.S. military cited *Rowland* as precedent, including four cases contesting policies that barred lesbians and gay men from serving in the armed forces.[7] As legal battles regarding same-sex marriage entered the courts in the 1990s, *Rowland v. Mad River* was cited in six cases, most notably *Windsor v. United States*, and twice in cases where same-sex partners sought equal access to civil protections and benefits granted to married couples. Litigants in these cases hammered out equal protection claims that were central to securing equal access to employment for LGBT educators, as illustrated in two cases involving teachers.[8] This chapter discusses LGBT cases involving serving in the military, same-sex marriage, and the right to teach.

The Opportunity to Serve

Gay men and lesbians have always served in the military but mostly without being open about their identity. For many decades, individuals known to be LGB or who were merely perceived to be homosexual were discharged, often dishonorably. Beginning in the 1980s, though, some LGB people fought for the right to serve in the military, and some of them used *Rowland* to help make their cases. In court cases regarding the right to serve in the U.S. military, dismissed lesbian and gay service members gained more traction with equal protection arguments than free speech arguments.

Of the four cases in the 1980s and 1990s that cited *Rowland*, only the first, *Johnson v. Orr*, relied primarily on a First Amendment claim. Significantly,

Johnson v. Orr was the only case among the four that the plaintiff lost (although another was overturned upon appeal). On June 24, 1983, First Lieutenant Julise M. Johnson sent a letter to her commanding officer to "clear the air," making her lesbian identity a matter of record. At the core of the letter, she wrote: "I am a lesbian and that will remain my political and sexual preference. However, my homosexuality does not in any way conflict with my ability to perform my military duties. I do not and will not advocate homosexuality to anyone while on military duty. I will continue to carry out my assignments and fulfill my commitments to the California Air National Guard."[9] Less than two weeks later, the air force initiated an administrative discharge, citing the regulation that mandates separation of homosexuals as unfit for military service. Johnson was honorably discharged in August 1984 and moved for a preliminary injunction requiring the U.S. Air Force Reserve and California Air National Guard to reinstate her. She argued that her dismissal violated the First Amendment free speech clause as well as article 1, section 8, clause 16 of the U.S. Constitution, which, she claimed, "precludes federal defendants from mandating the involuntary discharge of an officer in the California Guard."[10] The court dismissed both claims, giving most attention to the free speech argument.

District Judge Edward J. Garcia dismissed the free speech claim as specious, or lacking in merit, viewing "plaintiff's self-assertion of her homosexuality as nothing more than an admission of a fact, and such fact may serve as a lawful basis for discharge."[11] Johnson had maintained that the subsection of the regulation that led to her dismissal regulates pure speech and pointed to the finding of the Tenth Circuit Court in *National Gay Task Force v. Board of Education of the City of Oklahoma*, 729 F.2d 1270 (10th Cir. 1984) in support of her claim that such censoring was unconstitutional.[12] However, as discussed in chapter 1, the part of the Oklahoma law that the Tenth Circuit Court struck down involved advocacy; the court left intact the part of the law that called for homosexual teachers to be dismissed on the basis of their sexuality. Unfortunately for Johnson's legal case, she had explicitly stated in her letter to the commanding officer that she did not "advocate homosexuality to anyone while on military duty."[13] The fact that she had not spoken about her homosexuality while on duty weakened her argument for protection of free speech. Garcia concluded that Johnson's discharge "was not based on her advocacy of ideas, actions or conduct but rather, was based solely on her admission of a fact."[14] Further, Garcia ruled that Johnson's admittance regarding her sexuality failed the "public interest" test articulated in *Pickering v. Board of Education* and *Connick v. Meyers*, much in the same way the Sixth Circuit Court found against Marjorie Rowland. "The court finds in this case that plaintiff Johnson's letter to her commanding officer was a communication by an employee upon a matter personal to herself and was not a communication or advocacy of a citizen upon matters of public concern. Plaintiff's letter was particularized to herself, described her own homosexuality and stated that such sexual preference did not interfere with the performance of her duties."[15]

Johnson's district court hearing was held on November 7, 1984, just a few months before Justice Brennan issued his dissent in *Rowland v. Mad River*. Although Judge Garcia's decision was not filed until March 1985, he did not quote from Brennan's dissent on the free speech question of whether claiming a homosexual identity was a matter of public interest. Instead, Garcia relied upon the Sixth Circuit's finding that fighting for one's right to employment was not enough to stake a claim for free speech—even as he acknowledged the shifting political winds on employment discrimination. "This court fully agrees with the observation . . . that discrimination against homosexuals in employment is a matter of intense public debate and especially with respect to the military. . . . Had plaintiff Johnson made a speech espousing 'or denouncing' either side of the debate it would certainly appear that her comments would be protected by the First Amendment. However, plaintiff Johnson did not make such a speech."[16] Where Rowland's speech was at least in part for the purpose of helping two students, Johnson stipulated that she had not spoken about gay rights at all. Therefore, her letter could not be defended as an example of stating an opinion on a matter of public interest. The route to secure equal employment rights would have to come another way.

In 1989 two courts cited Justice Brennan's dissent in *Rowland* as they found in favor of soldiers facing discharge from the army on the basis of their sexuality. *Sergeant Perry Watkins v. United States Army* and *BenShalom v. Marsh* dragged on for years as the army blocked the reenlistment of Sergeant Watkins and Sergeant BenShalom. Both plaintiffs had voluntarily declared their sexuality status frequently during their years of service. The army relied on different regulations to support its action in the two cases: one that mandated the discharge of a soldier who "evidences homosexual tendencies, desire, or interest, but is without overt homosexual acts," and another that "mandated the discharge of all homosexuals regardless of merit."[17] In both cases, the LGB soldiers won, but BenShalom's victory at the district court was eventually overturned by the Seventh Circuit Court of Appeals. Watkins's victory was upheld by the Ninth Circuit Court.

Perry Watkins marked "yes" on the army's preinduction medical form asking if he had homosexual tendencies when he was drafted in 1967. Nevertheless, the army, mired in war in Vietnam, found him qualified for service. Watkins did not hide his sexual orientation, at times dressed in drag and performed as "Simone," and established an excellent record of service in the military. Battles over security clearances and reenlistments ensued throughout Watkins's career, and in 1982, an army board voted to discharge him on the authority of Army Regulation 635-200, chapter 15, which mandated separation of homosexuals regardless of merit. Before the discharge was processed, however, District Court Judge Barbara Rothstein ruled in favor of Watkins. The army then moved to block Watkins's reenlistment, and Rothstein enjoined that action, essentially blocking the army's block and requiring the army to allow Watkins to reenlist while the case proceeded. The army reenlisted Watkins for a six-year term with the understanding that the action would be void if the army won its appeal.

In 1983 (*Watkins I*) the Ninth Circuit Court reversed the district court opinion, finding that "the equity powers of the federal courts could not be exercised to order military officials to violate their own regulations absent a determination that the regulations were repugnant to the Constitution or to the military's statutory authority."[18] Under these guidelines, and with the antigay regulation not having been determined to be in violation of the Constitution, the district court found in favor of the army. When Watkins appealed that decision, a divided Ninth Circuit Court (*Watkins II*) reversed the most recent district court finding, holding that the army regulations on homosexuality did indeed violate the constitutional guarantee of equal protection of the laws. When the case was returned in 1988 to the Ninth Circuit en banc (meaning that all the judges in that circuit decided the case together), the majority again found in favor of Watkins on a procedural issue having to do with mixed messages the army sent over the years regarding Watkins's right to serve. This finding did not require the court to address the equal protection issues raised in *Watkins II*.

In a concurring opinion to the en banc decision, Judge William A. Norris, joined by Judge William C. Canby, argued that homosexuals constitute a suspect class under equal protection jurisprudence, addressing four critical points in the definition.[19] First, the group must have experienced a history of discrimination. On this point Norris noted that the army had already conceded to the standard set by Brennan: "Homosexuals have historically been the object of pernicious and sustained hostility."[20] Norris paired Brennan's critical observation with the more recent finding from the court in *High Tech Gays v. Defense Industrial Security Clearance Office*: "Lesbians and gays have been the object of some of the deepest prejudice and hatred in American society."[21] Norris then addressed a second factor in suspect class analysis, writing that discrimination against homosexuals embodies "a gross unfairness that is sufficiently inconsistent with the ideals of equal protection to term it 'invidious.'"[22] Here again, he referenced Brennan's dissent in *Rowland*. On the third point, Norris explained that, in looking to see whether the group in question manifests immutable traits that mark them for unfair treatment, the U.S. Supreme Court has never meant "that members of the class must be physically unable to change or mask the trait defining their class." Rather, "'immutability' may describe those traits that are so central to a person's identity that it would be abhorrent for government to penalize a person for refusing to change them, regardless of how easy that change might be physically. . . . With these principles in mind, I have no trouble concluding that sexual orientation is immutable for the purposes of equal protection doctrine."[23] Norris turned to Brennan's dissent in *Rowland* one more time, to secure the fourth point, showing that the group in question is "particularly powerless to pursue their rights openly in the political arena."[24]

The 7–4 decision rendered by the U.S. Court of Appeals for the Ninth Circuit in San Francisco in 1989 was the first ruling by a full appellate panel to strike down a ban on gay and lesbian service members. The George H. W. Bush administration appealed the case, but the U.S. Supreme Court did not take it under consideration. Rather than reenlist for a fourth time, Watkins settled the case and received retroactive pay, full retirement benefits, a retroactive promotion to sergeant first class, and an honorable discharge. He died in 1996 at age forty-eight from complications from AIDS.[25]

Sergeant Miriam BenShalom enlisted in the U.S. Army Reserve in 1974. Recognized as an excellent solider, she was nonetheless discharged two years later because she publicly acknowledged she was a lesbian. In 1980 a district court in Wisconsin held that the army had violated BenShalom's constitutionally protected rights to free speech, association, and privacy. The army dug in, refusing to reinstate Sergeant BenShalom on a technicality, arguing that the original regulation had been reworded. In 1987 the Court of Appeals for the Seventh Circuit dismissed this reasoning and directed the army to reinstate BenShalom, now over a decade since her discharge. The next year, at the end of her enlistment period, the army denied Sergeant BenShalom's reenlistment, citing revised regulations that made one's homosexual status a "'nonwaivable moral and administrative disqualification.'"[26] A district court once again considered BenShalom's claim against the army, finding that the regulation barring homosexuals from service violated free speech and equal protection claims. Similar to its finding in 1980, the court stated: "The Secretary has offered the court no basis to support the contention that acknowledgment of status equals reliable evidence of propensity. The court is asked to rely on the 'obvious connection' and to use 'commonsense.' In this context, the word 'commonsense' amounts to little more than a euphemism for prejudice. The court must decline to give such bias a sanctuary in our constitutional jurisprudence."[27] As in *Sergeant Perry Watkins v. United States Army*, the court cited Brennan's observations in *Rowland* that homosexuals have experienced a history of purposeful discrimination and lack the political power necessary to effectively meet invidious discrimination in the political sphere on its way to declaring homosexuals a suspect class in the equal protection argument.[28]

A major shift in military policy for LGB people came in 1994 with "Don't Ask, Don't Tell," a portion of the National Defense Authorization Act signed by President Bill Clinton. In an environment hostile to LGB people, this was an attempt to provide some minimal protection for gays in the military, yet it also perpetuated homophobia, did not challenge discrimination against gays and lesbians, and utterly silenced lesbian and gay service members. The policy assumed and seemed to accept the idea that gay men and lesbians were unwelcome in the military but said that if the gay and lesbian service members did not make their identities known, military officials would not ask and would not actively seek them out for dismissal. But three years later, in *Able v. United States*, a district court in New York found the "Don't Ask, Don't Tell" policy unconstitutional under the equal protection component of the Fifth Amendment.

The case had been sent back to the district court by the U.S. Court of Appeals for the Second Circuit with the direction to consider the constitutionality of both subsections of the act. In its first hearing, the district court had only considered subsection (b)(2) that required discharge of any service member who stated they were homosexual; it struck down the policy on the ground that it violated the First Amendment freedom of speech. The court did not believe plaintiffs had standing to contest subsection (b)(1), which required the discharge of service members who engaged in homosexual acts. The court of appeals, however, determined that the two subsections "rise or fall together" and sent the case back to the district court.[29]

As in the other cases we have examined, the district court referenced Justice Brennan's dissent in *Rowland* to substantiate that "homosexuals have historically been the object of pernicious and sustained hostility... reflect[ing] deepseated prejudice" and that homosexuals were "particularly powerless to pursue their rights openly in the public arena."[30] But in *Able v. United States*, Judge Eugene Hoffman Nickerson emphasized there was no need to *infer* from a history of discrimination against homosexuals. "Given the concessions by the government and the provisions of the Military Code, there can be no doubt that the purpose of the Act is to foster or at least acquiesce in the prejudice of some heterosexuals. . . . That prejudice was frankly announced in the congressional hearings. But the bleak history of discrimination against homosexuals in this country and elsewhere would in itself be sufficient to justify such an inference."[31] Judge Nickerson concluded with a reference to President Harry S. Truman's appeal to upholding "the highest standards of democracy" within the military when he signed the 1948 executive order to desegregate the armed forces. For his part, Nickerson added, "A Service called on to fight for the principles of equality and free speech embodied in the United States Constitution should embrace those principles in its own ranks."[32] In spite of the positive decision in this case, however, the "Don't Ask, Don't Tell" policy was not fully repealed until 2011.

Rowland's case, then, figured prominently in subsequent legal arguments regarding the rights of LGBT people to serve in the military. Not all the cases were resolved in favor of LGBT service members, but the arguments staked out in *Mad River* continued to sound the clarion call for civil rights. Similarly, Rowland's case furthered the cause of marriage equality.

The Right to Marry

A number of lower court judges adopted Justice Brennan's thinking on extending equal protection to LGBT citizens as they traversed the long road to marriage equality. One of those cases was *Snetsinger v. Montana University System*. The university system did not allow same-sex domestic partners to have the same employee insurance coverage that married couples in the system had. A district court sided with the university, but when the same-sex partners appealed in 2004, the Montana Supreme Court reversed the lower court decision, finding that the Montana University System policy violated the plaintiffs' rights to equal protection of the laws under article 2, section 4 of the Montana constitution. The reference to Brennan's dissent in *Rowland v. Mad River* appeared in Justice James C. Nelson's concurring opinion. He wrote to make the case that the Montana constitution "provides a stronger bulwark against the majoritarian oppression that gays and lesbians suffer daily in the State and for the claims under consideration here."[33] Nelson cited Brennan's statement that homosexuals lack sufficient political power to pursue their interests in the public sphere.

Several years later, Justice Nelson expanded that argument in *Donaldson v. State of Montana*. In this case, plaintiffs in committed same-sex relationships argued that a "statutory structure" in Montana law prohibited them from enjoying "significant relationship and family protections and obligations automatically provided to similarly-situated different-sex couples who marry." The plaintiffs sought a declaration that would acknowledge the State's failure to provide "equal protection, due process, and the rights to privacy, dignity and the pursuit of life's necessities" in accordance with article 2 of the Montana constitution.[34] The district court dismissed these claims, arguing that the declaration the plaintiffs sought was too broad, that to order the legislature to enact a "statutory scheme" to correct the inequalities in law would violate the separation of powers outlined in the Montana constitution. Further, the district court was averse to starting down a slippery slope of broad relief that might involve a number of other statutes. The Montana Supreme Court agreed with the lower court that a broad ruling or injunction in this matter was improper. The court predicted that, without specific attention to particular statutes, uncertainty about the laws and legal controversy would continue. Simply stated, the court declared, "Broadly determining the constitutionality of a 'statutory scheme' that may, according to the Plaintiffs, involve hundreds of separate statutes, is contrary to established jurisprudence."[35] In other words, each individual statute that discriminated against LGBT persons would have to be addressed separately rather than having one overarching case that took care of all of the many local and state laws and policies. The court majority noted that the plaintiffs could amend their complaint, develop an argument regarding specific laws they perceived as unconstitutional, and start over in the district court, essentially requiring a laborious and long process to secure equal treatment in Montana civil society. This decision was filed in December 2012, shortly before Justice Nelson retired in 2013 after twenty years on the Montana Supreme Court. As his last opportunity to address civil rights protections for gay and lesbian citizens from the bench, Nelson issued a 109-page dissent.

In writing his dissent, Nelson returned to an earlier case in which he had played a pivotal role. Nelson was the author of the majority opinion in *Gryczan v. Montana*, the 1997 case in which the Montana Supreme Court struck down state laws that criminalized gay sex, six years before the U.S. Supreme Court *Lawrence v. Texas* decision. Now, in 2012, he framed *Donaldson v. State of Montana* as the "most important civil rights case to come before this Court in decades," adding that he had "never disagreed more strongly with the Court as I do in this case."[36] Writing that the majority opinion took Montana civil rights backward, Nelson criticized the decision that required same-sex plaintiffs to "wage a litigation jihad against their own government to obtain the statutory rights, benefits, and protections to which they are constitutionally entitled."[37] Justice Nelson covered a lot of ground in his lengthy dissent. He applied Brennan's logic regarding the political powerlessness of gay men and lesbians to his argument that sexual orientation should be considered a suspect class under the Montana constitution and, therefore, claims involving discrimination should be subject to strict scrutiny review. Nelson questioned whether the majority decision could even be considered a token victory for the plaintiffs, because it would require considerable time, money, and fortitude to bring a series of new cases to successful conclusion in the courts. "Realistically the Plaintiffs here have gained nothing," he concluded. The problem was that the "Court has chosen to punt. And in simply kicking the can down the road, the Court has denied Plaintiffs the dignity, respect, fairness, justice, and equality to which they are entitled—foremost as human beings, and legally under Montana's Constitution."[38] In his dissent, Nelson carried forward the logic of Brennan's argument decades before in the *Rowland* case.

Judges also cited *Rowland v. Mad River* in cases that tested the constitutionality of laws prohibiting same-sex marriage, beginning in 1995. In *Dean v. District of Columbia*, the DC Court of Appeals upheld a lower court decision barring two men from legal marriage, although the judges' thinking diverged over whether homosexuals constituted a suspect class under the equal protection clause. In this case, Judge John M. Ferren cited Justice Brennan's dissent in *Rowland v. Mad River* to establish the point that homosexuals had, indeed, experienced a purposeful history of discrimination and to acknowledge that the U.S. Supreme Court had not yet addressed the suspect classification issue.[39] A decade later lower court decisions that supported same-sex marriage in Washington, California, and Maryland were overturned by divided appellate courts. The higher courts in Washington and California made a point of distinguishing between the law as written and a new legal standard that many in 2006 perceived on the horizon. "The time may come when California chooses to expand the definition of same-sex unions. That change must come from the democratic processes, however, not by judicial fiat."[40] In case after case, court majorities hesitated to break new ground on the suspect classification question, a critical turning point, always referencing Justice Brennan: "The closest any Justice has come to suggesting a view on the issue is found in *Rowland v. Mad River Local School Dist.*"[41] In 2008, however, another court moved in Brennan's direction. In Connecticut, a lower court ruled that the state was within its rights to prohibit same-sex marriage because the state allowed civil unions, and the court ruled that those state-sanctioned civil unions were good enough. But the Supreme Court of Connecticut disagreed and overturned the lower court ruling. In finding that "segregation of heterosexual and homosexual couples into separate institutions constitutes a recognizable harm," the Supreme Court of Connecticut ruled that homosexuals constitute a quasi-suspect class and that the state had failed to meet the associated standard of intermediate scrutiny.[42]

Disagreement over the appropriate level of review split the Second Circuit Court in *Windsor v. United States*, the critical ruling that set the stage for the landmark decision in support of same-sex marriage, *Obergefell v. Hodges*. In her case, Edie Windsor challenged the constitutionality of the Defense of Marriage Act (DOMA), the federal law that denied married gay couples legal recognition. In *Windsor* the appellate court majority struck down DOMA as unconstitutional because it violated equal protection rights. Section 3 of the act required the federal government to recognize only male-female couples as legally married, barring same-sex couples from the material benefits of civil marriage. Noting a lack of stability in previous court decisions regarding the appropriate standard of review in cases that addressed homosexuality and the law, the majority held DOMA to the standard of heightened scrutiny, finding that four criteria for quasi-suspect status held: (1) homosexuals have experienced a history of persecution and discrimination; (2) homosexuality has no connection to one's aptitude or ability to contribute to society; (3) homosexuals are a discernible group with nonobvious distinguishing characteristics; and (4) homosexuals are a relatively powerless political minority. The majority opinion cited Brennan's dissent in support of points 3 and 4.[43]

When the landmark DOMA case reached the U.S. Supreme Court, the justices passed on the opportunity to declare quasi-suspect status for LGBT citizens, even as a 5–4 majority found DOMA unconstitutional based on violation of the Fifth Amendment due process clause. Legal scholars have observed that courts may well extend a searching review—"rational basis with bite"—before they are ready to articulate a heightened level of scrutiny (whether intermediate or strict) for a new class of people. As Eric Berger explained, "Heightened scrutiny is not what the court says in these cases, but it may be what it does."[44] Justice Brennan was well ahead of the curve in this thinking, having suggested that LGBT citizens met the bar for suspect classification in Marjorie Rowland's case, some three decades before.

The Call to Teach

An openly bisexual person working in a school setting was at the heart of Rowland's case, and educators remain central to how her case has been used since then. Two cases involving teachers cited Justice Brennan's dissent in *Rowland v. Mad River*.[45] In one of those cases, that of Wendy Weaver, similar issues of speaking about one's identity was at issue. In the other, the teacher's self-identity was not the question; rather, the mere hint of "homosexual tendencies" was. In both cases, Brennan's dissent played a part in the defense of these teachers—defenses that, unfortunately, were not always successful. For Vernon Jantz, Brennan's dissent was used to deny him protection.

In *Vernon R. Jantz v. Cleofas F. Muci*, Jantz brought a 42 U.S.C. §1983 action against Muci, the former principal of Wichita North High School, alleging violations of Fourteenth Amendment equal protection rights. Jantz had taught continuously in various schools in the Wichita, Kansas, district but was twice rejected for full-time teaching positions. When he was not hired for an open position in 1988, Jantz, in a heterosexual marriage with two children, charged that the decision was rooted in prejudice against homosexuals even though he did not claim a homosexual identity. Deposition testimony from Muci's secretary and the director of social studies at the school indicated that Muci did not hire Jantz due to perceived "homosexual tendencies." The district court case resulted in a victory for Jantz that was overturned by the Tenth Circuit Court of Appeals. The appellate court found that Muci, the principal, was entitled to qualified immunity, which protects government officials from being held personally liable for violating anyone's civil rights. In reaching that decision, the court cited Brennan's dissent to establish the point that the courts were in disarray on the matter of discrimination based on homosexual or perceived homosexual orientation. The court also referenced *Bowers v. Hardwick*, the 1986 U.S. Supreme Court case that allowed states to define homosexuality as criminal. The appeals court in the Jantz case said, "Although the Hardwick Court did not deal with an equal protection claim, for qualified immunity purposes we think its holding, and the general state of confusion in the law at the time, cast enough shadow on the area so that any unlawfulness in Defendant's actions was not 'apparent' in 1988."[46] In other words, the principal could not be held accountable for a homophobic decision not to hire someone who may have struck him as gay because the courts had not given a clear message that such discrimination was illegal.

Ten years later, District Court Judge Bruce Sterling Jenkins spoke with clarity on the matter of constitutional rights of gay and lesbian teachers. In the spring of 1997, Wendy Weaver, a veteran teacher with an "unblemished" record, ran into trouble when her ex-husband (a school psychologist in the same district) began discussing her sexual orientation with Principal Robert Wadley and several members of the faculty in the Nebo School District, Utah. Gary Weaver's disclosures led to a cascade of complaints regarding Wendy Weaver's "lifestyle" as people made calls to other school officials, including Superintendent Dennis Poulsen. When Weaver, longtime winning coach of the girls' volleyball team at Spanish Fork High School, began preparing for the 1997 season, a member of the team asked her, "Are you gay?" Weaver responded yes, and the student said she would not play on the team because Weaver was a lesbian. The student and her parents then met with Almon Mosher, the director of human resources, and Larry Kimball, the director of secondary education, to report that the student would not play on a team coached by Weaver. Mosher and Kimball initiated action against Weaver, claiming that her comments about her sexual orientation violated district policy. In July, Principal Wadley informed Weaver that she would not be assigned to coach volleyball for the 1997 season and followed up with a letter that read, in part:

> The District has received reports that you have made public and expressed to students your homosexual orientation and lifestyle. If these reports are true, we are concerned about the potential disruption in the school community and advise you of the following:
>
> You are not to make any comments, announcements or statements to students, staff members, or parents of students regarding your homosexual orientation or lifestyle.
>
> If students, staff members, or parents of students ask about your sexual orientation or anything concerning the subject, you shall tell them that the subject is private and personal and inappropriate to discuss with them.
>
> This memo is to place you on notice of the expectations the school district has for you concerning this matter. A violation of these requirements may jeopardize your job and be cause for termination.[47]

On October 20, 1997, Weaver brought action under 42 U.S.C. §1983 challenging the restraints on her speech and removal as volleyball coach. On October 29 district officials sent a clarification letter to Weaver, stating that the restrictions outlined in the first letter "apply only while you are acting within the course and scope of your duties as a teacher for the District. Our main areas of concern are situations such as classroom teaching, extracurricular school-sponsored activities and parent-teacher conferences where, we believe, discussion of one's sexual orientation would be inappropriate. . . . We strongly encourage you to avoid discussions of the foregoing matters at any time with students because we believe that in virtually any interaction you have with a student, including off-campus contacts, you are always perceived by the student as a teacher, authority figure and role model."[48] Weaver claimed that the letters restricting her speech were overly broad and vague and, thus, constituted a violation of her First Amendment right to free speech. She also challenged her removal as volleyball coach as a violation of the Fourteenth Amendment equal protection clause.

With the facts of the case uncontested, Judge Jenkins found in favor of Weaver on both claims. He referenced Brennan's dissent to support the point on the free speech claim that "one's identity as a homosexual even though it is in essence a private matter is inherently a matter of public concern because it 'necessarily and ineluctably' involves that person in the ongoing public debate regarding the rights of homosexuals."[49] He continued, "It could be said that a voluntary 'coming out' or an involuntary 'outing' of a gay, lesbian, or bisexual teacher would always be a matter of public concern. Indeed, the public reaction in the Nebo School District to the rumors about Ms. Weaver's sexual orientation clearly evidence public concern over her sexual orientation."[50] Judge Jenkins spoke just as clearly on the equal protection claim: "Simple as it may sound, as a matter of fairness and evenhandedness, homosexuals should not be sanctioned or restricted for speech that heterosexuals are not likewise sanctioned or restricted for. Because the School District has not restricted other teachers in speaking out on their sexual orientation, the School District has not only violated the First Amendment, but also the Fourteenth Amendment's Equal Protection Clause."[51]

Judge Jenkins ordered that the warning letters be removed from Weaver's personnel file and that the Nebo School District offer her the coaching job and pay damages equal to the coaching stipend for one year. The school district did not appeal, sealing an important victory for LGBT educators and, by extension, the larger community. Jenkins struck an important chord on behalf of employment rights: "Although the Constitution cannot control prejudices, neither this court nor any other court should, directly or indirectly, legitimize them."[52]

It took five more years for the case to reach resolution, however. Shortly after Weaver filed her action in court, members of the Nebo community (students and other residents) began filing complaints with the school board, the school board's counsel, and the Utah Attorney General's Office, charging that Weaver had violated state statutes that govern the conduct of teachers and psychologists. On December 16, 1997, counsel for the school district informed the Citizens of Nebo School District for Moral and Legal Values that the school district would not act on its concerns within the time frame requested and clarified that the group must pursue civil litigation on its own. The civil case initiated by the Citizens of Nebo School District reached the Supreme Court of Utah in 2003. The court dismissed all counts due to a lack of legal standing, writing that the law "does not grant a private right of action to students and parents of students to enforce statutory and regulatory requirements for public school employees."[53] Rather, it fell to state authorized bodies (the local school district, the Professional Practices Advisory Commission established by the Utah Legislature in 1997, or the State Board of Education) to determine whether educators were morally fit to teach. Weaver's victory was allowed to stand.

Rowland's Legacy

A review of the imprint that *Rowland v. Mad River* made on the trajectory of the gay rights movement reveals some interesting considerations regarding the strategic use of the First and Fourteenth Amendments in laying claim to civil rights for LGBT citizens. As demonstrated in the analysis above, Rowland's case prompted courts to wrestle with the critical element of self-identifying speech in securing justice for lesbian, gay, and bisexual people. Brennan observed that "First Amendment and equal protection claims may be seen to converge, because it is realistically impossible to separate . . . spoken statements from . . . status."[54] As reasonable as that assessment appears, some courts parsed the public-private distinction in applications of First Amendment freedom of expression in ways that trapped bisexual, lesbian, and gay educators and members of the armed forces. To claim First Amendment protection for identifying oneself as a sexual minority, plaintiffs had to prove to the court's satisfaction that they were addressing a matter of public concern. Not all those sitting on the bench were as discerning in this regard as District Court Judge Robert Steinberg or Supreme Court Justice William Brennan. Perhaps they weren't as obtuse as the Sixth Circuit majority who saw no connection to public interest in Rowland's case. California District Judge Edward Garcia, for example, ended First Lieutenant Julise Johnson's hopes for continued military service due to the fact that she had not advocated explicitly for gay rights even though he understood that gay rights was, indeed, a contested issue. But demanding evidence of explicit advocacy from those in military ranks or working in public schools was asking too much. While school board members, officers in the military, and representatives in the U.S. Congress freely uttered discrimination and prejudice against LGBT people, LGBT educators and service members who publicly expressed their sexual identity knew that speaking out was a political act that would very likely cost them their jobs. As Judge Norris explained in his concurring opinion in *Sergeant Perry Watkins v. United States Army*, "Ironically, by 'coming out of the closet' to protest against discriminatory legislation and practices, homosexuals expose themselves to the very discrimination they seek to eliminate. As a result, the voices of many homosexuals are not even heard, let alone counted."[55] And then the federal government codified insistence on silence with the 1993 adoption of the "Don't Ask, Don't Tell" (DADT) policy (repealed in 2011). Law professor

Kenji Yoshino pointed out the absurdity of this compromised policy that guided legal policy for nearly twenty years. "So long as there is a *right to be* a particular kind of person, I believe it logically and morally follows there is a *right to say what one is.*"[56]

Notably, when the court considered the legality of the DADT policy it demanded that one's sexual identity status and free speech claims "rise or fall together."[57] Conversely, the highest court ruling on the fate of teachers' abilities to speak publicly on LGBT issues or claim an LGBT identity regarded the two issues as separate matters. When the U.S. Supreme Court reached a stalemate in *Board of Education of Oklahoma City v. National Gay Task Force*, 470 U.S. 903 (1985) it affirmed the Tenth Circuit Court opinion that struck down restrictions on speech. The U.S. Supreme Court said that the school district could not deny teachers the freedom to speak on LGBT issues. The Oklahoma law that allowed for the dismissal of lesbian and gay teachers, however, was not challenged.[58] In other words, the court in 1985 determined that it was acceptable for teachers to discuss homosexuality but that there was no protection for a teacher who *was* homosexual.

Another dimension of these court rulings has to do with the degree of consistency between an institution's core mission and the rights afforded its members. Courts have recognized the incongruity of the military failing to extend principles of equality and free speech to LGBT members within its ranks, when one of the armed forces' fundamental responsibilities is to protect and defend the Constitution of the United States. But in schools, widespread recognition of equal protection and free speech rights for LGBT educators remained elusive.[59] Ruthann Robson has pointed to a discordant juxtaposition of this lack of basic rights in school settings and the impact that has on academic freedom: "Unlike the military, which is an organization based upon discipline, educational institutions are based upon free thought and inquiry, often called academic freedom. This freedom supports an especially expansive reading of the First Amendment in the context of education."[60] While that logic certainly holds in principle, the reality for many LGBT educators remains contested, even with the 2020 Supreme Court decision that includes sexual orientation and gender identity in the definition of "sex" and, therefore, protects employees from discrimination.

Educational institutions claim a particular responsibility to the notions of free inquiry and debate. When school officials stifle speech and close off debate on LGBT issues, as they have done for decades, they betray the basic

principles of academic freedom. The legal scholar William Eskridge has written about the "pedagogical function" of the First Amendment, regarding
its "pluralistic commitment to tolerance."[61] In an analysis of Rowland's case,
he explained, "Expression to others of minority sexual orientation is uniquely
useful speech. . . . By coming out, openly gay people make a contribution to
the education of straight America."[62] Far from disrupting classroom learning, Eskridge argues, LGBT teachers add important dimensions to the
education that public schools can and should perform.

LGBT school workers—from Marjorie Rowland to Wendy Weaver to
those currently teaching—know that there is a price to be paid for that
kind of education. The Utah school officials who threatened Weaver relied
on the tired claim that LGBT teachers *became* a public controversy simply
by virtue of their status. In a deposition, Principal Wadley admitted that
the decision to strip Weaver of her coaching position was tied to her "controversial" status. He testified: "Wendy became within a very short period
of time, Wendy became a very controversial person in our community. . . .
And so Wendy went within a fairly short period of time, she became divorced
from her husband and moved in with a woman and announced you know,
public announcement, it became known that she had declared that she was
a lesbian. She became a very controversial person in town. And the reaction to that was generally negative."[63] Unlike Rowland's case, the Nebo
School District did not appeal the 1998 district court ruling in favor of
Weaver. Although Weaver won, the case came at a high cost to her; other
LGBT teachers may not want to open their lives to those challenges.

Alongside appreciation for the integrity, courage, and tenacity expressed
by LGBT educators who claimed First Amendment rights to claim their
identities publicly, it is important to acknowledge the limits of this route
toward equity. Cheshire Calhoun has made a vital distinction, noting that
"the first amendment protects speech, guaranteeing that some things *may
be said*. It does not protect speakers, guaranteeing that some sorts of speakers *may do the saying*."[64] Calhoun's instructive analysis of *Rowland v. Mad
River* leads to the conclusion that the central liberty at stake for Rowland
and countless other LGBT educators is the "liberty to conduct one's private
life" in a "public *nonpoliticized* space," in short, "to represent oneself as gay
or lesbian in the public sphere."[65] If the argument comes down to the right
to speak about LGBT issues, then LGBT people are "*debatable* speakers"
with "no social immunity from public scrutiny and public criticism."[66]
Under this framework, the right to live, work, and love as LGBT people

will, theoretically, always be up for debate. They cannot enter public life simply as teachers or citizens.

Theorists and legal scholars alike recognized the critical necessity of moving beyond First Amendment claims on LGBT rights before the U.S. Supreme Court reached that important breakthrough. Well before *Lawrence v. Texas, Obergefell v. Hodges*, and *Bostock v. Clayton County*, Paul Siegel predicted that "the moment that the gay liberation movement achieves liberation, the free speech claims will lose much of their force. Whatever vestigial and isolated pockets of homophobia and anti-gay discrimination that persist will then be combatted on more intellectually defensible grounds with privacy and equal protection arguments."[67]

The Supreme Court's 2020 *Bostock v. Clayton County* decision is hopeful, as the court determined that sexual orientation is included in Title VII's employment protection based on sex. But because the ruling was a narrow one that kept the burden of proof on those discriminated against and that allowed religious exemptions for discrimination, we may not see LGBT educators challenge discriminatory dismissals in the future. A robust embrace of academic freedom remains necessary to allow LGBT teachers and their students to participate in this unfinished revolution, without risk of losing their jobs.

"The wall between academic freedom and political expression," Judith Butler writes, "is porous; it is punctuated by windows and doors. The exterior light casts its shadow within, and the work inside often spills into the halls and into the streets outside."[68] Echoing other educators of times past, she underscores the reciprocal relationship between the free circulation of ideas within schools and the democratic society's obligation to protect that space for vibrant thinking, discussion, and being. Put simply, "the struggle for academic freedom belongs to the struggle for democracy."[69]

Brennan's dissent in Marjorie Rowland's case has had an enormous impact on civil rights cases for LGBT people involving service in the military, the right to marry, and, of course, the right to employment as educators. This chapter has looked at cases where the defense included reference to that dissent. Yet there were many other LGBT educators who fought for their right to teach, whose cases did not explicitly leverage that dissent. The next chapter turns to look at the experiences of educators since Rowland who have been fired, intimidated, or otherwise had to stand up for their right to be in classrooms.

4

"Coming Out of the Classroom Closet"

LGBTQ Teachers' Lives after
Mad River

> You can legally be married to the person
> you love, but you can't do the work
> that you love.

Marjorie Rowland's trial in 1981 occurred at a time when national politics
was taking a shift to the right: from the presidency of Democrat Jimmy
Carter to that of staunch conservative Ronald Reagan. The twelve Reagan-
Bush years, comprising Reagan's two terms followed by one term of his
vice president, hewed closely to Republican goals of smaller government
and trickle-down economics. On social issues, Reagan had campaigned for
a federal ban on abortion, the legalization of organized school prayer, and
an end to court-ordered busing.[1] And when a new disease suddenly appeared
that seemed to attack gay men, antigay forces had no trouble mobilizing to
further isolate and demonize lesbian, gay, and bisexual people. In spite of
the challenges, lesbian, gay, bisexual, and trans educators made some gains
during the decades following Rowland's case.

Developments in LGBTQ History

Date	Event
1940s	Federal government begins to purge actual and perceived homosexuals.
1950	U.S. Senate launches inquiry into employment of "homosexuals and other perverts" in government.
1950	Harry Hay founds first national gay rights organization, the Mattachine Society.
1952	American Psychiatric Association lists homosexuality as a sociopathic personality disturbance.
1953	President Eisenhower signs Executive Order 10450, restricting homosexuals from government employment.
1955	Del Martin and Phyllis Lyon found the first lesbian rights organization, the Daughters of Bilitis.
1959	Florida gives the state board of education investigative and subpoena powers to investigate teachers for homosexuality.
1961	Illinois becomes the first state to decriminalize sodomy.
1966	Compton's Cafeteria Riot—Transwomen and other LGBT people in San Francisco protest police violence and harassment.
1969	Stonewall Riots—LGBT people in New York City protest police violence and harassment.
1972	Teacher Jeanne Manford initiates idea for parent support group that would become PFLAG.
1973	American Psychiatric Association declassifies homosexuality as a psychiatric disorder.
1973	Maryland writes law banning same-sex marriage.
1974	National Education Association passes a resolution opposing discrimination on the basis of sexual orientation.
1977	Anita Bryant leads the Save Our Children campaign, targeting LGB teachers, among others.
1978	Briggs Initiative to ban LGB teachers and allies in California is defeated.
1978	Harvey Milk, first openly gay elected official in California, is assassinated.
1978	Oklahoma passes legislation banning gay and lesbian teachers and keeping all teachers from discussing gay issues.
1979	First National March on Washington for Lesbian and Gay rights.
1981	AIDS crisis begins.
1982	Wisconsin becomes the first state to ban discrimination on the basis of sexual orientation.
1984	Teacher Virginia Uribe establishes Project 10 in Los Angeles.
1985	Justice Brennan writes landmark dissent when U.S. Supreme Court chooses not to hear *Rowland v. Mad River*.
1985	U.S. Supreme Court upholds Oklahoma law banning LGB teachers but overturns the law banning teacher speech on LGB issues.
1986	U.S. Supreme Court rules in *Bowers* that states can criminalize same-sex acts.

Developments in LGBTQ History (continued)

Date	Event
1987	Second National March on Washington for Lesbian and Gay rights, especially regarding the AIDS crisis.
1988	Teacher Kevin Jennings and a student establish the nation's first gay-straight alliance.
1990	Kevin Jennings cofounds GLSEN (now known as the Gay, Lesbian, and Straight Education Network).
1993	U.S. Military begins "Don't Ask, Don't Tell" policy.
1996	Hawaii Supreme Court upholds marriage equality (state constitution amended in 1998 to ban same-sex marriage); U.S. Congress passes Defense of Marriage Act (DOMA), defining marriage as one man and one woman and stipulating that no state is required to recognize a same-sex marriage performed elsewhere.
2000	Vermont becomes the first state to legalize civil unions between same-sex couples.
2003	U.S. Supreme Court rules in *Lawrence v. Texas* that states cannot criminalize same-sex activity.
2004	Massachusetts becomes the first state to legalize gay marriage.
2008	California repeals its short-lived right for same-sex couples to marry.
2011	"Don't Ask, Don't Tell" is repealed.
2011	California is the first state to pass legislation requiring LGBTQ+ history in public schools.
2013	U.S. Supreme Court says that DOMA cannot deny same-sex couples federal benefits.
2015	U.S. Supreme Court declares same-sex marriage legal in all states.
2016	Pentagon lifts its ban on transgender people serving in the military.
2018	Transgender people are banned from serving in the military.
2020	U.S. Supreme Court rules that Title VII protection against discrimination in employment includes LGBT workers.
2021	Ban against transgender people serving in the military is once again lifted.

This chapter looks at the ways that life changed for LGBTQ educators in the 1980s, 1990s, and 2000s. The chapter discusses court cases won and lost, from the time of Brennan's dissent in the *Rowland* case to the landmark marriage case *Obergefell v. Hodges* in 2015. Not all issues end up in court; this chapter also looks at cases that were resolved without going to court. Over these decades, LGBTQ educators were harassed and fired but also experienced support and caring. Many states changed their laws to include employment protection for workers based on sexual orientation, and even in states without such laws, municipalities and school districts wrote nondiscrimination laws and policies, a major change over just a few decades. But problems remained. Attitudes do not always keep up with legislation, and teachers continued to face poor treatment even in states with nondiscrimination laws. Enforcing laws takes political will that sometimes is in short supply, and demanding enforcement of the laws sometimes is asking too much of a teacher who has reached their limit of harassment.

LGBTQ Educators' Rights from the 1980s to *Romer* (1996)

As we noted in chapter 1, during the years when Marjorie Rowland was waiting for a court date, two states voted on initiatives directed against lesbian and gay teachers. In California, the Briggs Initiative failed, but a similar piece of legislation passed in Oklahoma, Anita Bryant's home state. The bill, sponsored by the state senators Mary Helm and John Monks, allowed schools to fire teachers who were homosexual or bisexual, as well as those who, even though straight themselves, expressed the belief that nonheterosexual people were entitled to civil rights. An Oklahoma legislator who advocated for the bill said that it would allow school boards "to fire those who are afflicted with this degenerate problem—people who are deranged in this way."[2] According to some accounts, some administrators began firing teachers before the bill was even passed. The National Gay Task Force challenged the constitutional status of the bill on a number of grounds, arguing that it violated the right to privacy, equal protection under the law, and free speech.[3] This class action lawsuit was filed in October 1980, and in June 1982—about eight months after Rowland's victory at the lower level—the court upheld the law, saying that schools had a need to ensure that there was no disruption to the orderly conduct of the school. Two years later, the appeals court declared the part of the law that circumscribed speech unconstitutional—although it upheld the part of the law that barred homosexual teachers from employment. The ruling was a victory for free speech but not a victory for lesbian, gay, and bisexual teachers altogether. This case made its way to the U.S. Supreme Court in 1985, one month before the justices denied Rowland's petition for a writ of certiorari. A divided court upheld the appellate court decision.[4]

Two years later the court heard another case related to gay and lesbian rights: *Bowers v. Hardwick*. Although this case was not about educators, it had an impact on both civil rights and on the context in which schools made decisions. The case was about sodomy laws and privacy. A police officer had entered Michael Hardwick's home (the officer says a guest let him in) to deliver an outdated and invalid arrest warrant for failure to appear in court. (Hardwick had actually appeared and had paid his small fine for drinking in public.) Unannounced, the officer walked into the bedroom, where Hardwick and another man were having sex. The officer arrested them both on sodomy charges. This was in 1982, just months after Rowland's trial. Hardwick sued, hoping to have sodomy laws declared an unconstitutional violation of privacy. The lower court sided with the state of Georgia, upholding the law, but the appeals court reversed the decision. Georgia then took the case to the U.S. Supreme Court, where, in a close vote, the law was allowed to stand.[5] In other words, states could continue to legislate against certain types of consensual acts done in private.

The effect of the *Hardwick* decision was to give federal approval to state laws that "brand gay men and lesbians as criminals."[6] The decision also supported the prevailing social hierarchy that said that heterosexuals are acceptable and homosexuals are not. According to the legal scholar Christopher Leslie, the purpose of sodomy laws, even when they are largely unenforced, "is to condemn an entire class of Americans as immoral, inferior, and not deserving of society's tolerance and protection."[7] Criminalizing homosexuality meant giving school districts grounds not to hire known gays or lesbians and led many already-hired gay and lesbian teachers to stay in the closet for fear of losing their jobs. Catherine Lugg's analysis of the status of educators navigating a terrain bounded by sodomy laws and professional norms regarding licensure, morality clauses, and professional socialization emphasized the panoptic power of simply being watched. As Supreme Court Justice Thurgood Marshall observed in an unrelated case, "The value of a sword of Damocles is that it hangs—not that it drops."[8] The criminalization of homosexuality continued until *Lawrence v. Texas* reached the U.S. Supreme Court in 2003. But long before that happened, teachers kept fighting for the right to be themselves.

The *Hardwick* decision did not stifle all advances; nor did it keep teachers from pressing for being treated fairly and with dignity.[9] Arthur Lipkin was teaching at a public high school in Cambridge, Massachusetts, in 1987, the year after the *Hardwick* decision, when he faced harassment from another teacher. Lipkin already had faced harassment from students and others, including an incident in which someone wrote "and Lipkin" underneath the word "Ladies" on the women's restroom door. This time, a teacher had told a male student that if he took his pants off for Lipkin, Lipkin would give the student an A. This teacher had made other derogatory remarks for years, and Lipkin had had enough. Lipkin went to the principal's office, told him what had been said, and proclaimed that he "would stay home until gay teachers could be assured a safe workplace."[10] He stayed home for four weeks, until he could get a hearing with the superintendent. At this meeting, the harasser was represented by the union lawyer; because Lipkin was the one bringing the complaint, he had to find and pay for his own lawyer. Yet the superintendent sided with Lipkin. The harasser had a letter of reprimand put in his personnel file, and the superintendent agreed to Lipkin's demand for antihomophobia teacher trainings. The superintendent also issued antiharassment guidelines for the department. Two years later, in 1989, Massachusetts passed a statewide law banning discrimination on the basis of sexual orientation in housing, employment, credit, and access to restaurants and other businesses.[11]

Gary Campbell, a public high school teacher in Los Angeles, remembers being active in organizing for rights for lesbian and gay teachers in the 1980s. A group called Gay and Lesbian Educators of Southern California (GALE) had a mailing list of over three hundred people from Los Angeles and the surrounding areas, but in the 1980s, few of them were out. That group morphed into a new group, Gay Teachers of Los Angeles (GTLA), which Campbell led from 1983 to 1986. In 1987 Campbell helped launch the Gay and Lesbian Educators' Caucus of the National Education Association (NEA). Yet in spite of his activism, for much of the 1980s, he remained closeted at school. "I hated the days when I was in the closet," he wrote. "It made me feel inferior, isolated, and deceitful." Once he came out in the late 1980s, he felt "like a whole person."[12]

The year that the NEA began its Gay and Lesbian Educators' Caucus also was the first year of the National March on Washington for Lesbian and Gay Rights. The march was in part a response to the *Hardwick* decision, which had angered and disturbed many civil rights advocates. The march also was a response to the Reagan administration's continued lack of attention to the AIDS crisis. Park service officials estimated a crowd of at least 600,000 at the event. This was a huge act of visibility for LGBT people, and it did not end with the march. One long-lasting result was the organization of National Coming Out Day, launched on the one-year anniversary of the march in October 1988. As Gary Campbell wrote, "Think what could be done if we all came out!"[13] National Coming Out Day marked a strong push within lesbian and gay communities for everyone to be open about their sexual orientation. Many people found this inspiring and freeing.

One group of teachers inspired by the new push came out on the fourth National Coming Out Day, in 1991. Twenty-one teachers in the Los Angeles Unified School District met at the headquarters building and announced in front of television cameras that they were gay. In California, 1991 was an important year to take such a stand as Governor Wilson had just vetoed a bill that would have banned job discrimination on the basis of sexual orientation. The same day that these teachers came out at the school district headquarters, a protest of the governor's veto was held in Sacramento.[14]

In some districts and in some regions of the country, teachers did not face harassment and in fact found supportive communities. John Pikala, for instance, a public high school teacher in St. Paul, Minnesota, participated in a weekend retreat in Minneapolis for gay and lesbian educators in 1989. After the retreat, he came out to his principal and had no problem; he then came out to colleagues in his district. He became part of an activist group that built coalitions with other civil rights groups and put up a poster with pictures of famous gays and lesbians in his classroom that read, "Unfortunately, history has set the record a little too straight." In 1990 he walked with a large contingent of teachers in the Minneapolis Gay Pride march, noting that the teachers "received the loudest cheers from onlookers."[15] Even so, he also received harassing phone calls, including one from a person who shouted, "You dirty homosexual! You're going to hell! DIE!"[16] But for Pikala, the "few negative or indifferent reactions do not count for much compared with the overwhelming acceptance and support I have experienced."[17]

In 1994 a high school history teacher in Missouri came out to his students during a lesson on the Holocaust, a pedagogical decision that thrust him into the glare of the national media. Rodney Wilson had established a reputation as an excellent teacher who worked to make the study of history relevant to his St. Louis students. Wilson recalls getting the message as a young man growing up in the 1970s: gay people could not become teachers. But scholarly integrity won out in his efforts to teach students to respect the historical record. Wilson's simple statement that, had he been living in Nazi Germany, he would have been branded with the pink triangle, led to community uproar. Although Wilson was reprimanded for "inappropriate classroom behavior," many colleagues stood by his side, and support from the local chapter of the NEA was strong. He kept his job. That same year, Wilson founded the first Gay, Lesbian, and Straight Education Network (GLSEN) chapter outside of Massachusetts and established LGBT History Month, endorsed by GLADD, the Human Rights Campaign, the National Gay and Lesbian Taskforce, and the NEA.[18]

Administrators at an Oklahoma public high school in the early 1990s supported a lesbian teacher who was being harassed. Although the teacher welcomed the support, she believed it did not go nearly far enough. After weeks of being verbally harassed by one particular student, Ruth Irwin reached the breaking point when the student made gestures in class simulating a sexual act. Irwin had never come out to administrators, but when she wrote the student up for a discipline referral, she told the vice principal, "You need to know that he's harassing me because he thinks I'm a lesbian, *and you can't tell him I'm not.*"[19] The vice principal, who was new at his job, did not know how to respond to this, but fortunately he focused on the student's inappropriate behavior regardless of the orientation of the teacher. Irwin's experience is similar to Pikala in that, in both cases, the administration generally supported them. Their jobs were never at risk because of their sexual orientation. For Irwin, this is especially noteworthy given that her state of Oklahoma had passed the oppressive bill that made it legal to fire a teacher simply for advocating for civil rights for gays and lesbians; that bill had been found unconstitutional less than a decade before Irwin's encounter. While Irwin appreciated the support from her vice principal, that well-meaning support did not go quite far enough.

After this experience Irwin met with the vice principal and an assistant principal and, along with another gay teacher, began to talk about the teachers' lives at school. The administrators tried to assure the two teachers that they had confidence in them because "what you do outside of school has no effect at all on who you are as a teacher."[20] Irwin and the other teacher let them know that who they are had a great deal to do with their work lives. They told the administrators "about colleagues whose demeanor toward us would suddenly turn cold for no apparent reason; about anti-gay jokes we'd heard other teachers tell in the lounge and how that made us feel; about the colleague who insisted there were no gay or lesbian teachers in our district, and if he found out about any, he'd call the superintendent; about kids who yell names at us from a crowd in which they're hiding; about constantly pushing back the fear of losing the work we love."[21] The administrators were sympathetic and learned a lot, but this and subsequent conversations did not result in the writing of official policy regarding lesbian and gay teachers, and there continued to be no job protection in the district. The following year, some of those administrators left for other positions, and Irwin and her colleague were once again faced with "the task of trust-building with the new ones."[22] Irwin's example shows the hopefulness of changes in attitudes while also showing the sometimes very slow pace of that change. Irwin's story also demonstrates that the work involved in creating a supportive administration at the building or district level is not something that is done once and is achieved; it is something that requires repetitive effort.

In a New Hampshire school in the early 1990s, an incident of harassment did result in a significant administrative response. Rebecca went to school one day to find the word "DYKE" written on her desk calendar and the words "dyke from hell" written on a cup placed inside a file drawer. She went to the principal, who took the issue seriously. Together they planned a school diversity team that would work on racism, sexism, and homophobia, and the principal committed to bringing in guest speakers to address the school.[23]

By the 1990s, some states had passed laws protecting employees from workplace discrimination based on sexual orientation. As we saw in chapter 2, the first statewide law was the District of Columbia's in 1973 (covering all employment). This was followed by Pennsylvania's in 1975 and California in 1979 (both covering only state employment). In 1992 California broadened the scope of the law to include all employment. This had been a hard-fought battle, as Governor Pete Wilson vetoed a bill that would have made it illegal to discriminate against lesbians and gays in employment. When he announced his veto in October 1991, protests and demonstrations erupted across the state.[24] Wilson relented and signed similar legislation the following year. States passed laws protecting employees from discrimination on the basis of sexual orientation slowly in the 1990s. By 2000, only ten states had protections based on sexual orientation for state employees; another ten states plus the District of Columbia had those protections for all employees.[25]

At the same time, other cities and states mounted vigorous antigay campaigns, much like the legal battles in Florida, California, and Oklahoma in the late 1970s. In some of those states, there was not enough voter support for the antigay referendums to make it onto the ballot. But in four states, there was enough traction to put these questions before voters. In 1992 Oregon voters considered Measure 9, which would have amended the state constitution to say that no public funds could be used to promote "homosexuality, pedophilia, sadism, or masochism" and that the public school system must teach "that these behaviors are abnormal, wrong, unnatural and perverse and they are to be discouraged and avoided."[26] Although the measure was defeated, 600,000 people voted in favor of it, and after the defeat, more than two dozen cities and counties in the state passed similar versions of the law. All of those laws were eventually declared unconstitutional, which meant that the animosity generated by the debate went on for years as the laws went through the legal process.[27] In 1994, proponents of the bill tried again with a slightly toned-down version, also unsuccessfully.[28] In Idaho in 1994, citizens voted down a proposal to ban civil rights protections for lesbians and gays, prohibiting schools from teaching that homosexuality is acceptable and even limiting access to library materials that address homosexuality.[29] In 1995, 60,000 Maine citizens signed a petition to exclude homosexuality from protected status, which would have invalidated Portland's city ordinance prohibiting discrimination based on sexual orientation. The measure was defeated by a 6 percent margin.[30]

The fourth state to have an antigay measure on the ballot in the early 1990s was Colorado. This was the measure with the biggest impact—not only because it won but also because of the U.S. Supreme Court case that eventually resulted from it. When it passed in 1992, Colorado's Amendment 2 rescinded state and local nondiscrimination laws and prevented any future laws that might protect citizens on the basis of sexual orientation. The amendment stipulated that sexual orientation would not provide any protected status or any grounds for claims of discrimination. The amendment also made it impossible to "seek legislation, executive policies or judicial determinations protecting homosexuals . . . regardless of the merits of, or need for, such legislation, policies or determinations." This meant that there was no redress for discrimination.[31] As the educational historian Catherine Lugg put it, "Under this Orwellian legal construction, queers could be subjected to discrimination in every aspect of their lives, from housing, to employment, to education, to even buying a pizza. No part of one's life could be free from discrimination. And political action by queers to seek legal protections based on queer status was short-circuited by Amendment 2."[32] The amendment would have allowed school districts to fire educators on the basis of sexual orientation and would have prohibited teaching that homosexuality/bisexuality was acceptable. Just months after the amendment passed, a state trial court issued a temporary injunction preventing it from being added to the constitution until its legality could be determined. In June 1993 the Supreme Court of Colorado affirmed the injunction, and that December, on remand, the trial court found the amendment unconstitutional.[33] The Colorado Supreme Court affirmed, and *Romer v. Evans* went to the U.S. Supreme Court for a landmark decision.

When *Romer* was decided by a 6–3 margin in 1996, it established that lesbians, gay men, and bisexuals have the same right as any other group to seek protection against discrimination. The court also "rejected the notion that it is legitimate for the government to discriminate against gay people based on moral objections to homosexuality."[34] The court could find no rational justification for the amendment, concluding that "the Amendment raises the inevitable inference that it is born of animosity toward the class that it affects.... something the Equal Protection clause does not permit."[35] This was the first time in a decade that the U.S. Supreme Court had heard a case involving LGBT rights. The previous time was the *Bowers* decision in 1986, which had said that it was constitutional for states to criminalize sexual acts between same-sex consenting adults. Now, ten years later, the court was on record as stipulating that equal protection applies to gays and lesbians. The significance was enormous, and this case paved the way to the *Lawrence* decision that in 2003 finally decriminalized homosexual sex, seven years after *Romer*. The *Romer* decision also led to new ways to infringe on LGBT civil rights. Since the court found that states could not pass laws that curtailed one group's rights simply because another group found that first group abhorrent or immoral, tactics changed. Rather than write laws *against* LGBTs, states instead considered laws *for* protecting people who have religious or moral objections to homosexuality. Between 1993 and 2015, twenty-one states passed statewide Religious Freedom Restoration Acts.[36]

Courts and Beyond: Laws, Policies, and Practices

Although most states did not get proposed antigay laws on the ballot, and the only one to pass was ruled unconstitutional by the Supreme Court, having these issues front and center in public discourse often meant trouble for teachers, whether the laws passed or not. As Rita M. Kissen wrote, "Lesbian and gay teachers have been in the spotlight during all these campaigns. If they are implicitly or explicitly out, they become obvious targets for antigay rhetoric about pedophilia and 'special rights.' If they are relatively closeted, they are forced to listen silently to hostile remarks from some of their students and colleagues. And, in the climate of hate that referendum campaigns create, their fears of exposure often escalate to terror."[37] Teachers reported hearing an escalation of antigay rhetoric in their schools during these campaigns, including hearing references to concentration camps and executions and antigay epithets. After the amendment passed in Colorado, rumors swirled about a group collecting information on all unmarried teachers over the age of thirty in an effort to find—and fire—all the lesbian and gay teachers. It is possible that the conservative group Focus on the Family actually did call administrators asking for the names of all the single teachers in the building. True or not, the rumors had an effect. One teacher who had just joined a gay teachers' group "felt like Focus on the Family were sitting in cars with binoculars, writing down license plates. I was really afraid to do anything."[38] Kissen refers to these years as "teaching under siege."[39]

While some teachers were "under siege," other teachers lived in states with increasing protection. During the 1990s eight states passed laws banning discrimination based on sexual orientation in all employment (California, Connecticut, Hawaii, Nevada, New Hampshire, New Jersey, Rhode Island, Vermont), and five other states passed laws covering state employees only (Illinois, Louisiana, Maryland, Minnesota, Oregon). These laws were not always stable, though. Louisiana's law covering state employees was passed in 1992 and rescinded in 1996; Ohio's similar law was signed in 1983 and rescinded in 1999. Louisiana's protections would be reinstated in 2004, and Ohio's in 2007.

School districts also can have policies guaranteeing that teachers cannot be fired because of their sexual orientation. These policies are important, of course, but for some teachers they do not provide a sense of security. Two Massachusetts teachers who had statewide protection in Massachusetts in the early 1990s pointed out why they still had fears about coming out. "Lisa" noted that the law only works if one is willing to go to court to enforce it, and that takes both money and time. If you go that route, you might end up with a job, but you also might become known as "the one who rocked all those boats."[40] "Mary" felt that the state law was precarious and that she would not feel safe until federal protection was in place. Teachers in other states also reported that the protective laws did not make them feel safer because administrators could pressure teachers to resign or find other ways to fire them. "Bill" suspected that "they'd probably evaluate me to the point where they would be so nitpicky that I'd finally just say, 'I've had enough, good-bye.'"[41] Teachers feared that administrators, themselves pressured by parents or community members, would find ways to work around the nondiscrimination laws and get rid of gay and lesbian educators. This happened in the case of Michelle Serries, an openly lesbian teacher in Denver in the early 1990s. The principal wrote Serries up for such things as chronic lateness; she had been late for a total of three minutes over a four-month period, an infraction that surely would have otherwise been overlooked. After various incidents over several years, Serries resigned in 1993.[42]

Around the same time as Wendy Weaver's legal battle in Utah, other cases led to some degree of workplace protections. One of those cases took place in the town of Williamsburg, Ohio, about seventy miles south of Dayton, where Rowland had had her trial. Ohio had protection based on sexual orientation for state employees, a law passed by executive order in 1983.[43] Bruce Glover started out working as a long-term substitute teacher and received glowing reviews. When a permanent position opened up, the school hired him—like Rowland, on a one-year contract. During that year he was observed and evaluated, receiving high marks in all but two categories. "Management of student behavior" got a lower mark because Glover sent too many students to the principal's office. He also was marked down in "conformity to professional standards," based on an unsubstantiated rumor that Glover and his partner had held hands at a school holiday party. When Glover insisted that the hand holding had never happened, the principal investigated further and found that the rumor was indeed false; the principal then removed his comment about "indiscretions" from Glover's evaluation. Meanwhile, other parents complained to the school board, not only about the rumor of hand holding but also with a new rumor: that Glover's partner had visited the classroom. The principal checked out this rumor and found it too to be false but never told the board. During Glover's second semester, the principal again observed his classroom and evaluated his teaching. This time he gave Glover low marks on everything except "professional standards." That spring, Glover's contract was not renewed. Glover sued and won. In the 1998 trial, the court found that the low evaluations during the second semester, after the rumors began, merely gave the board a pretext for firing Glover and that the board discriminated against him because of his sexual orientation. The court noted that the board "did not present any evidence at trial to support a legitimate rationale for discriminating against homosexual teachers."[44] That is, the court would have accepted discrimination if there had been clear logic behind it; as it was, the board merely insisted that it had not discriminated. Glover was reinstated and awarded compensatory damages of over $71,000 for back pay and emotional distress.[45] The following year, unrelated to the case but in a move that no doubt would have had a significant negative impact, Ohio rescinded its nondiscrimination law.[46]

Courts increasingly were setting precedents for protections for teachers who spoke up about sexual orientation. In states with and without employment protections for lesbians and gay people, courts consistently upheld the right to free speech and due process. In 1999 a school district challenged the right to free speech for transgender teachers. David Warfield had been teaching for ten years in a California school district. A former navy electronics expert, a baseball coach, and a white-water rafting instructor, he also had won district and state teaching awards. In the late 1990s, he began transitioning to being a woman. In spring of 1999, Warfield sent a letter to colleagues and administrators letting them know that in the fall he would return to school as Dana Rivers. The district then sent a letter to parents informing them, making clear that Warfield/Rivers had tenure and was protected by antidiscrimination laws. Some teachers in the school read Warfield's letter to their classes, and students had questions. Warfield had conversations outside of class time with students who wanted to know more and gave an interview to the school newspaper. That summer, the school board placed Rivers on administrative leave until there could be a formal dismissal, which they said would happen soon. Rivers was not being fired, the board said, for being transgender, but for *talking* about it. Several parents had complained that "this teacher acted totally unprofessionally" and had "traumatized" the students by discussing his transition.[47] One parent went so far as to say that because her daughter heard the teacher talk about transitioning, "I felt my daughter was violated. I felt like somebody had raped my daughter."[48] Rivers argued that it was important to talk about it, given that the transition was not something that would be hidden from students; it would be obvious in the fall that David Warfield had become Dana Rivers. Rivers sued the school board for wrongful dismissal, based on the First and Fourteenth Amendments.[49] The school board settled rather than go to court, so we do not know what a court would have decided. Rivers retained her teaching license and went to another school district to teach.

While some courts upheld the right to free speech and due process, other courts opted not to protect openly gay teachers from harassment. In the early 1990s, sixth-grade teacher Tommy Schroeder came out at a public meeting in Wisconsin. After that, he began to experience harassment. Students hurled the "faggot" pejorative at him, shouted obscenities at him in the hallways and during bus duty, claimed that he had AIDS, made obscene phone calls to his home, and wrote explicit bathroom graffiti about him.[50] Schroeder reported the incidents, but administrators did not take much action, telling him that "you can't stop middle school kids from saying things. Guess you'll just have to ignore it."[51] When Schroeder asked the district to offer sensitivity training, the administration sent a memo telling teachers not to tolerate antigay slurs. To remove himself from the hostile environment, Schroeder transferred to an elementary school, but there he began to be harassed by parents. Someone slashed his tires, and he faced accusations of pedophilia. Still, administrators did not step in, and they actually made things worse. In response to the accusations—which were unsupported and unsubstantiated—the principal told Schroeder that he would not be allowed to be alone with any male students.

In 1998 Schroeder resigned in a state of nervous breakdown.[52] He subsequently sued the district, arguing that his right to equal protection under the Fourteenth Amendment had been violated. He lost the case at the trial level in 2001 and lost again on appeal in 2002 because the courts concluded that, while the district had not done everything possible to stop the harassment, the district had done what was required. In addition, even if Schroeder had been treated differently than straight colleagues, the court decided that the district would have been justified in doing so. One judge explained this decision by saying that there is no way to stop antigay harassment without talking about homosexuality and that would be inappropriate because "it will make children prematurely preoccupied with issues of sexuality."[53] Therefore, the state (in the form of the school district) had a rational interest in preventing such talk. Another judge explained the decision by saying that the equal protection clause does not apply: "Homosexuals have not been accorded the constitutional status of blacks or women," who are covered under the equal protection clause.[54] Schroeder appealed to the U.S. Supreme Court, but it declined to hear the case. Unlike Rowland's situation, no justice wrote a dissent.

The *Schroeder* outcome came on the heels of another Wisconsin case that had a very different result. In that case, an openly gay student named

Jamie Nabozny had been harassed, bullied, and assaulted by classmates for years. One time, he was beaten so badly that he had internal bleeding and needed surgery. He and his parents went to school administrators for help, but, as with Schroeder, Nabozny was told that "boys will be boys" and that there was not much anyone could do. In addition, one administrator told him that if he had not come out, this would not be happening to him. Nabozny finally moved to another state to finish his high school education. He sued the school district in Ashland, Wisconsin, in 1995, and, in spite of the evidence of the horrific treatment he endured, the court found for the district. The judge ruled that a school district cannot be held liable for the actions of students. When Nabozny appealed the case, the court ruled in 1996 that districts do have an obligation to protect students and remanded the case to the lower court. This time, the court found for Nabozny, and the district settled for $900,000.[55]

Nabozny was a landmark case establishing schools' obligation to protect all students, including gay and lesbians; it occurred in the same state as the *Schroeder* case and was settled five years before Schroeder sued his district. The district in the *Nabozny* case had used some of the same defense arguments that the district used in the *Schroeder* case—that a district was not responsible for students' behavior. Those arguments fell apart in the appeal of the *Nabozny* case, yet the defense in *Schroeder* used the same logic. And in the *Schroeder* case, that defense worked. The major difference was that in *Nabozny*, a student was harassed and abused, and in *Schroeder* the target was a teacher. Schroeder's district argued that it had no obligation to protect employees from that type of treatment, and two of the three appellate judges agreed. The third judge, Diane P. Wood, lamenting the outcome of the case, wrote, "There is no dispute that Schroeder was a very good teacher; he taught successfully for the District for 22 years. . . . [Yet] he left the school . . . a ruined man."[56] One of the greatest ironies of these two cases is that the state of Wisconsin was in the forefront of having laws that prohibited discrimination on the basis of sexual orientation and required school districts to have written nondiscrimination policies in place.[57] Such laws are necessary—crucial, even—but clearly are not sufficient.

As we have seen, the *Bowers* decision in 1986 affirmed the constitutionality of anti-sodomy laws. This meant that states could choose to criminalize same-sex acts between consulting adults. In the 1990s, many states dropped those laws. But in 2003, fourteen states still had anti-sodomy laws. Where states had these laws, school districts had justification for dismissing gay and lesbian teachers who were found guilty of breaking those laws. Conviction also could mean having to register as sex offenders, being required to note the conviction on job applications, being denied the right to adopt children, and, of course, suffering a sense of stigma and loss of dignity.[58] This changed when the U.S. Supreme Court decided in *Lawrence v. Texas* that anti-sodomy laws were not constitutional. The court based this decision on two principles: the right to privacy without government intervention, under the due process clause of the Fourteenth Amendment, and the principle that the state could show no legitimate state interest to justify the violation of privacy.[59]

The *Lawrence* decision was a major victory for gays, lesbians, and bisexuals, as engaging in private consensual sexual acts no longer meant being a criminal. But this ruling did not immediately change attitudes, and, in fact, the ruling led to a backlash against civil rights for lesbians and gay men.[60] Almost immediately after the ruling, President George W. Bush felt that "traditional marriage" was so in need of defense that he advocated a constitutional amendment banning same-sex marriage.[61] He carried this theme into his campaign for a second term, making opposition to same-sex marriage part of his platform.[62] In the first decade of the twenty-first century, then, gay and lesbian people were free from the fears of being rendered criminals because of their sexual orientation, had gained protections in many states, and had witnessed more liberal views in the broader culture. But they also faced a backlash that saw civil rights for LGBTQ people as in direct opposition to a particular set of morals and values. In 2004 alone, thirteen states passed state referendums banning gay marriage.[63] Marriage laws changed in 2015 nationally, finally allowing lesbians and gays in every state to marry.

Making Tough Choices

In the midst of all of these legal battles over civil rights, gays and lesbians continued to teach. Often teachers have to make tough decisions about how open to be about their sexual identity, regardless of whether their states or school districts have nondiscrimination policies. The sociologist Catherine Connell found surprisingly little difference in teachers' classroom lives when she studied teachers in California, a state with such policies, and Texas, a state without statewide nondiscrimination laws (although some counties and districts had nondiscrimination policies). In her 2008 study, teachers reported incidences of dismissals that occurred immediately after coming out to administrators, but because other reasons were given for the dismissal, discrimination was hard to prove. A teacher who posted a picture on Facebook of himself at a Pride march was asked not to teach for the rest of the year. Other teachers reported constantly engaging in toning down any markers of being gay or lesbian and worried that, in a coteaching environment, no straight teacher would want to teach with them.[64]

An example of the way that school climate can have more impact than statewide nondiscrimination laws is the case of Julia Frost. Frost taught high school for two years in Southern California, a state with strong nondiscrimination laws. Although she had an excellent first-year review, in 2012 she was fired (or had her contract nonrenewed) in her second year, just days after she gave a student a form on which the student could file a complaint of harassment. The student was alleging a pattern of homophobic slurs from other teachers. The effort to file this complaint occurred in a year in which the administration censored Gay/Straight Alliance club announcements of meetings over the school's public address system and omitted the club from the student handbook. Frost was one of the faculty advisers for the Gay/Straight Alliance but the only openly lesbian one. She, but not the straight adviser, was repeatedly called into the principal's office to be questioned about alliance activities, and she was told she was "being investigated for 'teaching homosexuality.'"[65] Frost believes that she was fired because she was a lesbian and because she encouraged gay and lesbian students to speak out against harassment and discrimination.[66]

Frost's case had not yet been settled at the time of this writing, but another teacher who was fired after speaking up negotiated a partially successful conclusion. Brett Bigham had the honor of being named the 2014 Teacher of the Year by the Oregon Department of Education and the 2015 Teacher of the Year by the Oregon Education Association. Bigham is openly gay. His school district ordered him not to talk about being gay during any of the addresses he gave or meetings he held during his year of statewide talks. When he did anyway, and when he took a personal day to meet with a Gay/Straight Alliance, the district fired him. "My district had sought to silence me," Bigham wrote. "They also felt LGBT teachers had no value—even if they were the Teacher of the Year."[67] Facing media pressure, the district offered him a $160,000 settlement if he would resign and drop his threat of a lawsuit for discrimination and harassment. Bigham agreed. The supervisor and superintendent who had issued the gag order and who had fired him were themselves dismissed. Since then, Bigham has spoken nationally on antibullying issues for LGBTQ students.[68]

Connell concluded that nonheteronormative teachers choose among three paths, which she termed "splitting," "knitting," and "quitting." Splitting entailed leaving one's sexual identity at home and positioning oneself as an asexual person in the classroom. For many, this meant that they could have the teaching career they valued and could also have their private lives away from school where they could inhabit their sexual identities. This approach had a cost, however. One cost was the constant fear of being found out by someone at school, for instance, if a student or another teacher saw them give a loving touch or glance at their partner at some public setting away from school.

A second cost was having that split identity, not being able to talk about one's personal life or issues with friends or colleagues at work. As Jasmin Torres explained, "You are constantly thinking about what you're saying, what you're not saying, whether you're giving anything anyway. You become hyper-aware of how people perceive you." As a result, she said, "I was lonely."[69] Professor Rita M. Kissen wrote that "hiding is a constant strain. It prevents [educators] from forming authentic relationships, from turning to colleagues in moments of joy or distress, from feeling that they are truly known for the people they are. Most of all, it renders them invisible."[70] This was a cost Marjorie Rowland was unwilling to pay when she told her secretary that the reason she was so happy was because she was in love with a woman. For "splitters," not revealing personal information is worth it to keep their jobs.

A third cost that several teachers in Connell's study described was feeling like hypocrites. These teachers saw LGBTQ students in their schools struggling with their identities and with the pain of harassment and ostracism. The teachers knew what difference it might make for those students to have an out role model, as studies have shown the importance of role models. In addition, straight students could gain a different conception of what being LGBTQ means if they see it embodied in their teachers. For splitters, then, there are clear benefits as well as costs to keeping their identities out of the classroom.

Teachers who do not want to split their personal and professional worlds often choose to be what Connell calls "knitters." As the term implies, these educators knit their personal and professional identities and are visible in their schools as lesbian, gay, bisexual, trans, or queer people. People who do this do not have the stress of being inadvertently outed by someone else, and they do not have the stress of leaving part of themselves out of their professional setting. They also can feel good about being a role model to youth. On the other hand, for many educators who go this route, there are costs for doing so. Many experience harassment from students, colleagues, or parents. Even when there are policies that should protect employees, no policy can stop every instance of harassment. Some educators who come out also feel that their being LGBTQ becomes the predominant aspect of their identity; it becomes the primary way they are thought of and talked about in the school. In addition, no one comes out all at once to everyone. It is an ongoing process that can require constant negotiation and assessment of the context. Connell also found that most LGBTQ educators who are knitters also are white, demonstrating the role that race can play in this decision. For LGBTQ educators of color, who operate "from a location of multiple marginalities," deciding whether, when, and where to come out also requires considering the ways that race factors into their situation.[71]

Finally, for educators who are uneasy about coming out or who have been harassed after coming out, quitting is the logical choice when the other options become untenable. A 1987 study of gay teachers found that, of those who left teaching, fully half cited their sexuality as the reason.[72]

Carla Hale's experience illustrates the difficulty of being a splitter— having one identity inside the classroom and another identity outside of the classroom. Hale taught for many years in a Catholic high school in Columbus, Ohio, where she did not discuss her private life. But when her mother died in 2013, the obituary listed Hale's longtime partner as one of the survivors. A parent at the high school saw the obituary and brought it to the attention of officials within the diocese. Hale was fired. Similarly, an assistant principal in a Catholic high school in Cincinnati, Ohio, was fired in 2013—not for being gay but for writing positively about gay marriage in a personal blog post.[73]

Conclusion

For many LGBTQ people and their allies, the U.S. Supreme Court decision in 2015 that made same-sex marriage legal everywhere in the United States was a major victory. Many activists were stunned, never believing they would live to see this. Celebrations were plentiful. But as often happens with a political move in one direction, a backlash ensued. In states without nondiscrimination laws, a gay or lesbian person could get married but then also could get immediately fired from their jobs. This happened to several teachers. A high school music teacher in Georgia, Flint Dollar, was fired after posting on his Facebook page that he planned to get married. He had taught in his Catholic school for four years and "was told very specifically I didn't do anything wrong, that there were no parent complaints, no student complaints, but regardless, I would not be returning."[74] In St. Louis County, Missouri, a teacher was fired from his job at a Catholic school when the archdiocese learned that he was marrying a man.[75] In another case that underscores the uncertain terrain that lesbian, gay, and bisexual teachers walk, Archbishop Charles C. Thompson ordered two Roman Catholic schools in Indianapolis to fire gay teachers who had recently married. At Cathedral High School, officials eventually fired a teacher they had defended as maintaining an exemplary record after their months-long appeal failed to move the archbishop from his ruling. Officials at Brebeuf Jesuit Preparatory School, however, maintained their defiance of the archbishop's order on the grounds that firing the teacher at their school would violate "our informed conscience on this particular matter."[76] The two teachers from the same archdiocese were married to each other.

Exactly what protections teachers have in private schools, religious or not, is most likely an issue that will come up in the future given the push for so-called religious freedom laws. These laws emerged in the early 1990s, gained strength as gays and lesbians began to get more civil rights, and have garnered national attention in the wake of the *Obergefell* case. How this all plays out remains to be seen. What we do know, though, is that lesbian and gay educators will continue to teach—and will continue to face their own dilemmas about whether or not to come out to colleagues and students. Whatever decisions they make, the repercussions will be determined by a mix of factors, including the microclimate in their schools, community context, and the degree to which administrators abide by the nondiscrimination mandate handed down by the Supreme Court in *Bostock v. Clayton County*. In the next chapter, we look more closely at the current situation for LGBT educators.

5

Movements Forward
and Back

I treasure this dissent. I was seen and I
was heard, and it wasn't just me, it was
the message that I was trying to carry
out there.

Marjorie Rowland's story is remarkable in some ways and not at all in other
ways. It is remarkable because her case made it all the way up to the U.S.
Supreme Court; there, Justice Brennan's dissent laid the foundation for so
many other cases advocating civil rights for LGBTQ people. Rowland's case
helped set precedent, which is crucial in the path toward legal protection.
Rowland was courageous in suing the district that, according to the trial
court, discriminated against her by not renewing her contract. She was
relentless in pursuing justice in spite of receiving threatening calls at home
and even when local officials retaliated by charging her with food stamp
fraud. She continued the fight all the way to the top court in the country.
She pursued her case while raising three small children, going to law school,
supporting women fighting domestic abuse, and counseling teenagers at
risk of substance abuse. She succeeded in getting her town of Yellow Springs
to pass an ordinance that included sexual orientation in the definition of

"sex" so that LGBTQ people had protection against discrimination. Her persistence, her courage, and her accomplishments are remarkable.

Seen in the context of all the other brave educators who took enormous risks to claim civil rights for themselves and other LGBTQ educators, Rowland's story becomes less singular. She is part of a barely visible throng, all working to end discrimination against LGBTQ teachers, principals, and counselors. As we have shown in this book, Rowland was not alone. She was one of many educators who, from the 1970s until today, have fought to keep their jobs despite of (or because of) their sexual orientation or gender identity. One of the saddest things is that in most instances, none of these impressive educators knew about those who came before. In what ways might each of them have been bolstered or have found wells of courage in knowing the stories of others who had fought similar battles? This is one of the main purposes of this book: to get these stories to those who need to hear them.

LGBTQ teachers and their allies continue to have much work to do in spite of the ruling in *Bostock v. Clayton County* that struck down employment discrimination on the basis of sexual orientation and gender identity in 2020. Some LGBTQ educators remain closeted for fear of losing their jobs, and the protections, based on Title VII of the 1964 Civil Rights Act, do not appear to reach educators working in parochial schools.[1] Under these conditions, academic freedom remains at risk at best, and stifled altogether at worst. Where educators' very jobs are under threat, the school climate for gender nonconforming students is likely to be intimidating and unwelcoming. This chapter provides a brief overview of the range of these issues in our schools today.

Protecting LGBTQ teachers' rights is essential not only for the well-being of educators; it is also a critical step toward creating and maintaining safe learning environments for LGBTQ students in elementary and secondary schools. Initially prompted by student activism in Gay/Straight Alliances, findings from a 1989 Health and Human Services report on youth suicide, and the 1996 *Nabozny v. Podlesny* ruling, school officials and state lawmakers have made uneven progress on this front, as illustrated by the broad range of specificity in antibullying legislation and in the widespread variation in how policies are implemented. Research suggests that in spite of these laws, there has been little change in the culture of schools.[2] More recently, actions by the Trump administration eroded federal policy regarding transgender students and exacerbated disputes over who can use which bathrooms—disputes that can make schools hostile if not dangerous places for some students. In 2014, the Departments of Justice and Education stipulated that transgender students were covered under Title IX. But in 2017, the Trump administration rescinded that guidance, effectively saying that "the federal government is no longer instructing schools that they have an obligation to treat transgender students with the same dignity as any other students, including when it comes to bathroom access, and that the government . . . may not fully enforce Title IX's protection."[3] In addition, the Department of Health and Human Services attempted to establish a narrow definition of sex as "either male or female, unchangeable," essentially erasing the identities of anyone who identifies as transgender, gender fluid, or nonbinary.[4] This narrow definition, which one neuroscientist called "an insult to science," would have far-reaching negative repercussions for many students, including an increased potential for violence.[5]

Nationwide, there has been a rise in violence against LGBTQ people. The FBI recorded a 17 percent increase in all hate crimes in 2017, including over 1,200 based on sexual orientation or gender identity. In 2018 the Human Rights Campaign documented twenty-six deaths of transgender people due to violence, most of these attacks on Black transgender women. The trends are not abating, prompting the American Medical Association to issue a warning of "an epidemic of violence" against transgender people of color.[6] The increase in reports of violence parallel significant changes in the Gay and Lesbian Alliance against Defamation (GLADD) "Accelerating Acceptance" study conducted by the Harris Poll. Americans age eighteen to thirty-four were the only age group to show a decline in acceptance of LGBT people: 63 percent reported they were comfortable interacting with LGBT people in 2016, 53 percent in 2017, and 45 percent in 2018. A third of this age group were uncomfortable with LGBT teachers, and 39 percent opposed LGBT lessons in the curriculum.[7] For the first time in a decade, the Gay, Lesbian & Straight Education Network (GLSEN) 2017 National School Climate Survey indicated that victimization of LGBTQ youth is *not* decreasing at rates previously set, and the trend is getting worse for transgender and gender nonconforming youth. Still, 87.3 percent of LGBTQ students report experiencing harassment or assault based on personal characteristics (sexual orientation, gender expression, gender, religion, race and ethnicity, disability).[8] Progress toward the basic civil rights goals of safety and recognition is incomplete. And as Catherine Lugg observed in 2003, "protection or non-oppression is not the same as social justice or, for that matter, education."[9]

In many postsecondary institutions, LGBTQ students now can see themselves represented in their courses of study. The University of Nebraska offered the first gay studies class in 1970, and California State University, Sacramento, established the first gay studies program two years later. Scholarship in gay/lesbian/queer studies has proliferated since the 1990s, and hundreds of colleges and universities offer courses, certificate programs, minors, majors, and graduate degrees in sexuality studies. In a 2013 assessment, Jasmina Sinanovic wrote, "While graduate education in gay/lesbian/queer studies seems to remain remanded to existing disciplines in which students working with established scholars can pursue sexuality as a subfield . . . several campuses around the country are establishing gay and lesbian studies programs to facilitate the distribution of knowledge in the undergraduate curriculum."[10]

Despite the presence of LGBTQ studies programs and courses in colleges and universities, teacher education programs tend not to address these issues. As Frank Dykes and John Delport note, "LGBTQ issues are often marginalized" in teacher preparation programs.[11] Even in teacher preparation courses designed to prepare teachers on multiculturalism, LGBTQ issues seldom are represented in meaningful ways. One study of eighty people who teach multicultural courses found that LGBTQ concerns often were invisible in the courses or were covered in ways that continued to center heterosexuality.[12] Once teachers enter schools, they seldom receive professional development on LGBTQ issues.[13] An attempt in California to require public school teachers to receive training on these issues failed, primarily over the objections of conservative religious groups and families. A second bill, encouraging rather than mandating such training, passed in 2019 requiring the state Department of Education to make training resources available by 2021.[14] Administrators can play key roles in creating school cultures that are healthy for LGBTQ students, yet few administrators receive much training on this issue.[15] A study of university principal preparation programs found that LGBTQ issues are "nearly absent from the literature on leadership preparation."[16]

The curricular landscape in elementary and secondary schools is even more stark. Despite pioneering efforts such as Project 10, launched in Los Angeles in 1984, the U.S. Surgeon General's call for AIDS education in 1986, and the ill-fated Children of the Rainbow curriculum in New York (1992), curricular decisions regarding LGBTQ issues remain at the discretion of local districts in most states. GLSEN's National School Climate Survey has consistently found that schools with curriculums inclusive of LGBT issues are less hostile toward LGBT students, yet in 2017, 64.8 percent of students surveyed reported that LGBT issues were not addressed in the curriculum. About half of the students who noted that their schools addressed LGBT issues in the curriculum (19.9 percent of the full sample) perceived that the issues were addressed in a positive manner, while 18.6 percent reported that LGBT issues were addressed in a negative way.[17] In 2016, only seven states mentioned the terms *lesbian, gay, bisexual,* and *transgender* in their state standards for social studies.[18] The connection between curriculum and student safety has been established by such education scholars as Mollie Blackburn and C. J. Pascoe, who point to ways in which LGBTQ-inclusive curriculums, antibias curriculums, and queer pedagogy interrupt homophobic and heterosexual oppression and make schools better places for LGBT students.[19]

Five states have mandated that school curriculums include LGBTQ history and culture. California was the first state to do this, in 2011. New Jersey, Colorado, Oregon, and Illinois have passed similar laws. California's law requires that schools include study "of the roles and contributions of lesbian, gay, bisexual, and transgender people in the history of this country and State" and requires that textbooks bought with state funding cannot include content that is discriminatory.[20]

However, other states' laws go in the opposite direction and mandate that teachers keep LGBTQ lives invisible to students. So-called no promo homo laws in Alabama, Arizona, Louisiana, Mississippi, Oklahoma, South Carolina, and Texas "explicitly prohibit the positive portrayal of homosexuality in schools."[21] In South Carolina, homosexuality cannot even be discussed in health education class, except for the purpose of instruction related to disease. Even in states where public schools are required to include LGBTQ history and culture, many students in those states never receive that content. Although California passed its law in 2011, the first LGBT-inclusive textbooks for classrooms were not approved until 2017. While LGBT content could have been included before textbooks were available, one LGBT ally reported seeing "a lot of schools dragging their feet."[22] Private schools, whether religious or not, usually are exempt from these laws.

Embracing a curriculum that introduces students to the gay liberation struggle and invites them to raise questions about sexuality and social justice still requires its own kind of advocacy. It requires a commitment to the principles of academic freedom that protect inquiry, debate, and hard questions. But as we noted in chapter 3, in securing this basic academic principle, we need to be aware of the problem of relegating LGBTQ rights to "free speech" arguments alone. After all, everyone has a claim on free speech, including politicians, school officials, and community members who cast LGBTQ people as immoral beings. If the validity of LGBTQ teachers' visibility in school rests only on speech that someone can challenge, a free speech argument can just as easily be used to dismiss them.[23] Teachers, too often, are not afforded the most basic nods to academic freedom, the right to be, think, and educate beyond narrow boxes of intellectual and social convention. And teachers are the key.

As the historian Jackie Blount has established, the ranks of educators have always included people who, today, might identify as LGBTQ—those who desired persons of the same sex or otherwise transgressed conventional gender norms.[24] For much of the last century, these educators engaged strategies that kept their sexual and gender identities hidden, for fear of losing their jobs—or worse—in periods defined by intense discrimination. Blount describes the history of LGBT educators as "complex ... replete with secrecy, with fear about how gender and sexual norms will pass from one generation to the next, with moments of opportunity and praxis, and finally, with an open call to acknowledge our existence and better understand our circumstances."[25]

The gay liberation movement sparked by the Stonewall Riots was a clear turning point: "Prior to Stonewall the majority of LGBT people hoped to be left alone[,] to avoid persecution and prosecution. After Stonewall LGBT people formed visible communities devoted to pursuing political agendas that made demands rather than asked for recognition."[26] LGBT teachers came out in larger numbers after Stonewall. A few teachers joined the public demonstrations and annual Pride parades that began in 1970, at times with paper bags over their heads to hide their identity. In his 2019 dissertation, Jason Mayernick explains that teachers were among the first LGB workers to organize to fight against discrimination. They formed local organizations in at least eight cities—Boston, Baltimore, Chicago, Denver, Los Angeles, Portland, San Francisco, New York—and established caucuses in the National Education Association and American Federation of Teachers. Many of the leaders of these teachers' groups were also actively engaged in the broader gay liberation movement.[27]

In this context some individual educators who had been fired because of their sexuality or gender identity were stirred to challenge the unjust actions in court, leading to high-profile cases in the 1970s and 1980s. Marjorie Rowland was among this determined group. Collectively, these legal challenges slowly coalesced into a patchwork of laws that provided improved, if uneven, employment protections across the nation—although the teachers involved in the cases rarely were able to return to the classroom. Educators also found themselves thrust into the center of the political firestorm that engulfed the early success of antidiscrimination laws in the 1970s, most notably in Florida, California, and Oklahoma. Antigay activists targeted LGBT teachers, among all workers, in their efforts to obstruct equal access to employment.[28] These battle lines were (largely) abandoned, abruptly, with the onset of AIDS in the 1980s as the whole of the gay rights movement threw its effort into fighting the disease. In schools, attention shifted to protecting LGBT students. Gay politics in the 1990s were characterized by state initiatives written to advance or curtail civil rights for LGBT Americans. In this climate of state initiative after state initiative, the impact on LGBT teachers was deeply felt, regardless of the particular outcomes of the extended debate, as hostility toward LGBT teachers was on full display.

The most critical legal advance for LGBT Americans came in 2003 when the U.S. Supreme Court ruled sodomy laws unconstitutional. At that time, fourteen states and Puerto Rico still prohibited private, consensual homosexual activity between adults, meaning that LGBT educators could be denied state teaching credentials or fired due to their status as statutory felons.[29] Shortly after *Lawrence v. Texas* was handed down, the legal scholar Laurence Tribe described it as the gay and lesbian parallel to *Brown v. Board of Education*. And he reminded readers of one of the lessons from *Brown*: "We cannot assume that society's acceptance of such watershed decisions—decisions that mediate revolutions in the entrenched social order—will be a straightforward and predictable process."[30] Indeed, the vital act of striking down legal mechanisms that branded LGBT citizens *criminal* did not lead directly to *civil* rights, such as equal access to employment. The amici briefs that the Williams Institute filed in *Bostock v. Clayton County* present a wealth of information documenting the contemporary extensive reach of employment discrimination.[31] LGBT educators remain vulnerable in this hostile climate.

Teachers occupy the most influential positions in schools; as the education historian Paul Violas put it, nothing happens in the classroom that does not pass directly through their hands. This is in spite of a history in the

United States that, largely, has denied teachers due regard for professional autonomy. The feminization of teaching in the nineteenth century left a legacy that still affects how some view the profession—as if nurturing the development of children and adolescents required little more than honing gendered traits supposedly rooted in biology. Dominant models of teacher preparation circulate regularly back to a primary focus on training characteristic of normal school origins, emphasizing particular pedagogical techniques and behavior management rather than a broader foundation in liberal education.

Complicating the situation, schools serve a diverse constituency. Those who have entered the ranks of teachers have worked under the scrutiny of a public that understands that what children learn in school has a hand in shaping the future. Given the wide range of perspective in the United States about what that future should entail, teachers—by political necessity if not a philosophical commitment to democratic community—learn to make their way carefully around controversial curricular topics. They must weigh varying perspectives and read social context as they carry out their academic responsibilities.[32] This is challenging work under the best of circumstances. When teachers' very beings signal a shift in bedrock cultural understandings of gender and sexuality, the teacher becomes part of the curriculum. That teacher's ability to transmit cultural understanding is challenged. The paradox that James Baldwin spelled out in his "Talk to Teachers" is made clear:

> The paradox of education is precisely this—that as one begins to become conscious one begins to examine the society in which he is being educated. The purpose of education, finally, is to create in a person the ability to look at the world for himself, to make his own decisions, to say to himself this is black or this is white, to decide for himself whether there is a God in heaven or not. To ask questions of the universe, and then learn to live with those questions, is the way he achieves his own identity. But no society is really anxious to have that kind of person around. What societies really, ideally, want is a citizenry which will simply obey the rules of society. If a society succeeds in this, that society is about to perish.[33]

This possibility of coming to our own terms about identity, society, and the things that matter distinguishes schools from other conservative institutions. A shared function of these institutions is to stabilize the social order.

Regardless of how committed they may be to particular types of social training and transmitting established culture, however, there's always the chance that schooling might lead to the kind of education that disrupts the social order. It seems obvious; the fear of thinking in new ways about gender and sexuality, this instability in the school terrain, provokes lingering intense reactions against LGBT educators. Put another way, an increasing visibility of queer teachers might very well ignite a kind of cultural power reminiscent of that generated by the early Pride parades that stepped off fifty years ago. As the embodiment of a queer presence in school, might teachers, finally, now lead the way toward a more inclusive curriculum and safer schools for LGBTQ students?

Analyzing the twenty-first-century dilemma facing queer teachers can be a vehicle for wrestling with circumstances confronting the teaching profession generally. Will LGBTQ teachers be protected by *Bostock v. Clayton County* on the ground, in the schools where they work? In districts that resist the Supreme Court decision, teachers are also likely to lack the full academic freedom they need to expand the curriculum to address LGBTQ issues. Without that, all students' civic education suffers, and they are less equipped to continue the struggle for social justice, however each one perceives that challenge. As the teacher and activist Margaret Haley famously asserted in 1904: "There is no possible conflict between the interest of the child and the interest of the teacher.... For both the child and the teacher freedom is the condition of development. The atmosphere in which it is easiest to teach is the atmosphere in which it is easiest to learn. The same things that are a burden to the teacher are a burden also to the child. The same things which restrict her powers restrict his powers also."[34]

Consider, too, the teachers' ability—if not responsibility—to claim academic freedom, the freedom to teach, to the extent possible in any given historical moment. To be sure, conditions are constantly shifting and require strategic flexibility in terms of action. Nonetheless, teachers should be vigilant for those "moments of opportunity and praxis" to advance equity in education.[35] Academic freedom is a cornerstone of promoting equity, as it models the very citizenship that we want students to engage in. Speaking freely about momentous issues in a way that promotes critical thinking, and challenging accepted conclusions in ways that stimulate thoughtful debate, is exactly how educators can best serve a democratic state.

Marjorie Rowland's story matters in part because her story is not over. The same battles she fought—for the right to her job, for the right to

FIG. 5.1 Marjorie Rowland, 2019

visibility for LGBTQ faculty and students, and for teachers' protection under First Amendment rights to free speech—continue to be waged today. Although LGBTQ rights and visibility have increased greatly since the *Mad River* case, there still is a long way to go. LGBTQ people have attained critical legal protections. LGBTQ characters now are present on television shows and movies, and many prominent figures, especially in the entertainment industry, are publicly out. A majority of U.S. citizens support gay marriage. But as these advances have been made, those in opposition to such rights have become more vocal. Some major Protestant denominations have split over the issue, creating splinter groups based on views of LGBTQ people, while more fundamentalist groups have hardened their stances in opposition to any rights or protections. In areas where these groups predominate, LGBTQ educators and students will likely face great pressure.

Why did Marjorie Rowland become an activist? What makes any citizen stand up for their rights against what must feel like insurmountable odds? She was a single mother of three small children; she needed her job and the income it provided. So one answer is simply that she was fighting for her livelihood. If that were the entire answer, she might have quit one year, two years, three years, or six or ten years into the battle when she had found other work. But she did not quit. Her fight was grounded on principle: that someone should not lose their job—in her case, a job she was performing well and in which she was helping LGBTQ students who needed support—simply because of whom she loved. Rowland was someone who saw, perhaps, interlocking oppressions. She did not fight only against the injustice perpetrated against her. Rather, she had a history of fighting racial segregation and of protecting victims of domestic violence. Her life history of activism is one of fighting multiple types of oppression, reflecting the knowledge that allowing one type of injustice clears a path for other types of injustice.

Rowland's fight for fairness for herself as a bisexual guidance counselor failed in the short term. She did not get her job back, and she felt repercussions from her standing up for justice long into her career as a lawyer. But through her fight, she planted important seeds that have taken root. Her fight led to the brilliant dissent written by Justice Brennan, a dissent that has laid the groundwork for much of the civil rights for LGBTQ people that followed. Because of her courage and the courage of scores of other LGBTQ educators who have taken mighty risks, the cause of equity has advanced enormously since her case began. This is her legacy.

Acknowledgments

Our first debt of gratitude goes to Marjorie Rowland, for having the courage and determination to fight for her right to be employed in a school system. We are deeply grateful to her for her activism and for her willingness to spend time telling us her story.

The History of Education Society (HES), our primary professional organization and a strong and supportive intellectual home, has been foundational in advancing our research on LGBTQ education, including this study. We presented aspects of this work at HES annual meetings and benefited from insights and suggestions offered there. Colleagues who have been especially helpful on this project are Lucy Bailey, Nancy Beadie, Jackie Blount, Tim Cain, Linda Eisenmann, James Fraser, Michael Hevel, Patti Lather, Yoon Pak, Sevan Terzian, Marc VanOverbeke, and Joy Williamson-Lott. We would also like to acknowledge colleagues in the American Educational Research Association, the International Standing Conference for the History of Education, the Organization of American Historians, and the Southern History of Education Society for their thoughtful commentary on portions of this research. Some material in chapter 1 was first published as "Staking a Claim in Mad River: Advancing Civil Rights for Queer America," in Doris A. Santoro and Lizabeth Cain's edited volume, *Principled Resistance: How Teachers Resolve Ethical Dilemmas*.

Our thanks to our editors, Lisa Banning, William Rarich, Kimberly Guinta, and Ben Justice, at Rutgers University Press for their support of this project.

Karen would also like to acknowledge the Denison University Research Foundation for two grants that funded parts of the research. Many thanks are due Cheryl Johnson, instructional technologist at Denison, for her patient technical support. Denison students Kelsey Schwimmer and Hannah Wedepohl provided research assistance during different phases of the work. Colleagues at Denison in educational studies, queer studies, and women's and gender studies have been generous with their knowledge, queries, and critiques regarding this work. BeJae Fleming and Mary Tuominen are two great listeners; conversations with them often reveal previously unconsidered nuances in my thinking. It has been my great pleasure to collaborate on this project with my friend and colleague Maggie Nash. Her scholarly depth, insight, and capacity for storytelling brought a critical focus to our analysis of one woman's journey and refined our writing on an experience shared by far too many educators. Finally, my profound thanks to Sharon Flynn—for a lot, including her untiring encouragement to "tell it like it is!"

Margaret would also like to acknowledge the Graduate School of Education at the University of California, Riverside, for providing a supportive academic environment for this and other work. Thanks to Begoña Echeverria for feedback on chapter drafts. Deepest thanks to Karen Graves for inviting me to be part of this incredible project. We were talking about our current work over lunch at a conference when she first introduced me to the story of Marj Rowland's legal battles and what they meant. We had no idea then that this would turn into a book or that we would spend time in Tucson getting to know Marj. Karen is simply the best coauthor and colleague anyone could wish for. I am grateful to have been part of this project and delighted that together we have told an important story and along the way deepened a friendship that I treasure. The work on this book has been inspiring, uplifting, maddening, and heart wrenching as we have learned the details of Marj's and other LGBTQ educators' fights for justice. Endless thanks to Susan Harlow for love, laughter, and adventures.

Notes

Chapter 1 Staking a Claim in Mad River

Epigraph: *Rowland v. Mad River Local School Dist.*, 470 U.S. 1009, 1014, (1985).

1   In this book, we use various terms to refer to lesbian, gay, bisexual, transgender, queer+ people, in parallel with the shifting, fluid terminology regarding sexual orientation and gender identity. In historical analysis, we draw on language used by people at the time. In contemporary analysis, we apply more inclusive queer+ language. Given our focus on educators who defined themselves as lesbian, gay, bisexual, or transgender, we use *LGBT* most often.

2   Matt Tedeschi, "Somewhere over the Rainbow? What the *Bostock* Decision Means for the LGBT Community," Prinz Law Firm, accessed February 16, 2021, https://www.prinz-lawfirm.com/our-blog/2020/june/somewhere-over-the -rainbow-what-the-bostock-deci/.

3   Herron Walker, "Here's Every State that Requires Schools to Teach LGBTQ+ History," Out, accessed December 18, 2020, https://www.out.com/news/2019/8 /16/heres-every-state-requires-schools-teach-lgbtq-history.

4   Shabab Ahmed Mirza and Frank J. Bewkes, "Secretary DeVos Is Failing to Protect the Civil Rights of LGBTQ Students," Center for American Progress, accessed December 18, 2020, https://www.americanprogress.org/issues/lgbtq-rights /reports/2019/07/29/472636/secretary-devos-failing-protect-civil-rights-lgbtq -students/; Avery Anapol, "DeVos Defends Controversial Guidance on Transgen-der Students," The Hill, accessed December 18, 2020, https://thehill.com /homenews/administration/438257-dem-asks-devos-if-she-knew-of-potential -harm-to-transgender-students; Luke Broadwater and Erica L. Green, "DeVos Vows to Withhold Desegregation Aid to Schools over Transgender Athletes," *New York Times*, September 18, 2020, https://www.nytimes.com/2020/09/18/us /transgender-students-betsy-devos.html; Dave Zirin, "Betsy DeVos Attacks Trans Athletes Again," *The Nation*, October 23, 2020, https://www.thenation.com /article/society/trans-devos-title-ix/.

5   Jackie M. Blount, *Fit to Teach: Same-Sex Desire, Gender, and School Work in the Twentieth Century* (Albany: State University of New York Press, 2005), 60–78.

6   Alfred Kinsey, Wardell Pomeroy, and Clyde Martin, *Sexual Behavior in the Human Male* (Philadelphia: W. B. Saunders, 1948).

7   David K. Johnson, *The Lavender Scare: The Cold War Persecution of Gays and Lesbians in the Federal Government* (Chicago: University of Chicago Press, 2004); Beth Bailey, *Sex in the Heartland* (Cambridge, MA: Harvard University Press, 2002); Margaret A. Nash and Jennifer A. R. Silverman, "'An Indelible Mark': Gay Purges in Higher Education in the 1940s," *History of Education Quarterly* 55, no. 4 (November 2015): 441–459.

8   See James A. Schnur, "Closet Crusaders: The Johns Committee and Homophobia, 1956–1965," in *Carryin' On in the Lesbian and Gay South*, ed. John Howard (New York: New York University Press, 1997), 132–163; Karen L. Graves, *And They Were Wonderful Teachers: Florida's Purge of Gay and Lesbian Teachers* (Urbana: University of Illinois Press, 2009); Stacy Braukman, *Communists and Perverts under the Palms: The Johns Committee in Florida, 1956–1965* (Gainesville: University Press of Florida, 2012); Robert Cassanello and Lisa Mills, dirs., *The Committee*, DVD (Orlando: University of Central Florida, 2015, 2016), https://www.pbs.org/show/committee/; Judith Poucher, *State of Defiance: Challenging the Johns Committee's Assault on Civil Liberties* (Gainesville: University Press of Florida, 2014).

9   Graves, *And They Were Wonderful*, 10–12.

10 Braukman, *Communists and Perverts*.

11 Sodomy laws are laws that define certain sexual acts as illegal, usually because the legislators define those acts as immoral. Those acts have varied by state and period but usually include oral and/or anal sex. Sodomy laws usually concern sex acts between consenting adults, as other laws, such as rape and assault laws or laws determining age of consent, cover acts between nonconsenting adults or sex with minors.

12 Blount, *Fit to Teach*, 108–155; Fred Fejes, *Gay Rights and Moral Panic: The Origins of America's Debate on Homosexuality* (New York: Palgrave Macmillan, 2008); Karen Graves, "Political Pawns in an Educational Endgame: Reflections on Bryant, Briggs, and Some Twentieth-Century School Questions," *History of Education Quarterly* 53, no. 1 (2013): 1–20; Karen M. Harbeck, *Gay and Lesbian Educators: Personal Freedoms, Public Constraints* (Malden, MA: Amethyst, 1997), 39–81.

13 Richard Steele and Holly Camp, "A 'No' to the Gays," *Newsweek*, June 20, 1977, 27, http://o-www.lexisnexis.com.dewey2.library.denison.edu/hottopics/lnacademic/.

14 Cited in Joyce Murdoch and Deb Price, *Courting Justice: Gay Men and Lesbians v. the Supreme Court* (New York: Basic Books, 2001), 252. See also, Karen Graves, "Sexuality," in *Miseducation: A History of Ignorance-Making in America and Abroad*, ed. A. J. Angulo (Baltimore: Johns Hopkins University Press, 2016), 53–72; Harbeck, *Gay and Lesbian Educators*, 83–98.

15 Cited in Murdoch and Price, *Courting Justice*, 255.

16 Blount, *Fit to Teach*, 108–134.

17 Murdoch and Price, *Courting Justice*, 176–180; Blount, 116–118; Harbeck, *Gay and Lesbian Educators*, 248–257.

18 Murdoch and Price, 196–198; Blount, 118–120; Harbeck, 258–263.

19 Cited in Harbeck, 266.
20 Murdoch and Price, *Courting Justice*, 241–246.
21 Murdoch and Price, 241–246.
22 Murdoch and Price, 237–240; Linda Greenhouse, "Supreme Court Roundup; Case Refused for Bisexual in Loss of Job," *New York Times*, February 26, 1985, http://www.nytimes.com/1985/02/26/us/supreme-court-roundup-case-refused-for-bisexual-in-loss-of-job.html; Glen Elsasser, "Supreme Court Keeping Silent in Cases Involving Gay Rights," *Chicago Tribune*, March 4, 1985, http://articles.chicagotribune.com/1985-03-04/news/8501120683_1_supreme-court-justices-william-brennan-highest-court.
23 Murdoch and Price, *Courting Justice*, 239.
24 Elsasser, "Supreme Court Keeping Silent." The Supreme Court took up its first gay rights case involving education, *Board of Education of Oklahoma City v National Gay Task Force*, the next month. The difference: had they denied cert. in this case, a pro-gay ruling would stand.
25 *Rowland v. Mad River Local School Dist.*, 470 U.S. 1009, 1011, (1985).
26 *Rowland v. Mad River Local School Dist.*, 470 U.S. 1009, 1012, (1985).
27 *Rowland v. Mad River Local School Dist.*, 470 U.S. 1009, 1013, (1985).
28 *Rowland v. Mad River Local School Dist.*, 470 U.S. 1009, 1013, (1985).
29 *Rowland v. Mad River Local School Dist.*, 470 U.S. 1009, 1012, (1985).
30 *Rowland v. Mad River Local School Dist.*, 470 U.S. 1009, 1014, (1985).
31 *Rowland v. Mad River Local School Dist.*, 470 U.S. 1009, 1015–1017, (1985).
32 Graves, *And They Were Wonderful*, 20–49.
33 Notably, teachers who work in parochial schools and employees of other institutions that claim a religious exemption to antidiscrimination laws are not covered by the ruling in *Bostock v. Clayton County*.
34 "Marjorie H. Rowland v. Mad River Local School District, Montgomery County, Ohio, 470 U.S. 1009 (1985)," *Court Listener*, n.d., https://www.courtlistener.com/opinion/111388/marjorie-h-rowland-v-mad-river-local-school-district-montgomery-county/.
35 Stephen L. Sepinuck and Mary Pat Treuthart, eds., *The Conscience of the Court: Selected Opinions of Justice William J. Brennan, Jr. on Freedom and Equality* (Carbondale: Southern Illinois University Press, 1999), 126.
36 Wiemann v. Updegraff, 344 U.S. 183, 196, (1952).

Chapter 2 "I Had to Be the Fighter"

Epigraph: Marjorie Rowland, interview with author, July 28, 2016.

1 Mad River Local Schools, homepage, accessed September 6, 2017, https://www.madriverschools.org/.
2 "Dayton, Ohio," City Data, accessed September 6, 2017, http://www.city-data.com/city/Dayton-Ohio.html.
3 "Paul L. Dunbar," Ohio History Central, accessed September 6, 2017, http://www.ohiohistorycentral.org/w/Paul_L._Dunbar.
4 "Dayton, Ohio," Ohio History Central.
5 "Dayton, OH," Atomic Heritage, accessed September 6, 2017, http://www.atomicheritage.org/location/dayton-oh.

6   Robert Mueller, "Wright-Patterson Air Force Base," in *Air Force Bases, Vol. I: Active Air Force Bases Within the United States of America on 17 September 1982* (Washington, DC: Office of Air Force History, 1989).

7   Diane Chiddester, *Two Hundred Years of Yellow Springs* (Yellow Springs, OH: Yellow Springs News, 2005).

8   Marjorie Rowland, interview with author, July 28, 2016.

9   Marjorie Rowland, interview with author, July 28, 2016.

10 Marjorie Rowland, interview with author, July 28, 2016.

11 Petition for Rehearing with a Suggestion for Rehearing En Banc Submitted by Plaintiff-Appellee Marjorie Rowland to the Sixth Circuit U.S. Court of Appeals, no. 82-3218, p. 2.

12 Marjorie Rowland, interview with author, July 28, 2016.

13 Marjorie Rowland, interview with author, July 28, 2016.

14 "Teacher Claims Ruling Ignored," *Xenia Daily Gazette*, March 8, 1975, 12.

15 Petition for Rehearing, p. 3.

16 "Teacher Files New Suit over Contract," *Xenia Daily Gazette*, June 3, 1975, 13.

17 Rowland v. Mad River Local School District, #76-2450, Sixth Circuit Court, 1977, summarized in "Opinion of the Trial Court," U.S. District Court for the Southern District of Ohio, Western Division, case no. C-3-75-125, p. 2.

18 "Homosexual Counselor Loses Bid to Regain Job," *Xenia Daily Gazette*, August 23, 1977, 5.

19 "Summary Judgment," *West's Encyclopedia of American Law*, 2nd ed., accessed September 11, 2017, http://legal-dictionary.thefreedictionary.com /summary+judgment.

20 "Homosexual Counselor Loses Bid to Regain Job," 3.

21 Marjorie Rowland, interview with authors, June 20, 2017.

22 "Dayton, Ohio, Judge Voids a Busing Plan," *New York Times*, Dec. 16, 1977, http://www.nytimes.com/1977/12/16/archives/dayton-ohio-judge-voids-a-busing -plan-says-naacp-failed-to-provide.html.

23 Marjorie Rowland, interview with authors, June 20, 2017.

24 The trial ran from September 30, 1981, until October 15. Arguments regarding damages and liability extended until October 22. Arguments regarding attorney fees extended for months.

25 Marjorie Rowland, interview with authors, June 20, 2017.

26 Marjorie Rowland, interview with author, July 28, 2016.

27 Marjorie Rowland, interview with author, July 28, 2016.

28 Gretchen Millich, "East Lansing Marks 40th Anniversary of Gay Rights Ordinance," WKAR, March 6, 2012, http://wkar.org/post/east-lansing-marks -40th-anniversary-gay-rights-ordinance#stream/0.

29 William N. Eskridge, *Gaylaw: Challenging the Apartheid of the Closet* (Cambridge, MA: Harvard University Press, 2009), 130.

30 "Gay Rights Incorporated in Very Unusual Manner," *Mansfield News-Journal*, July 5, 1977, 3.

31 Benjamin E. Widener, "Sex Discrimination Includes Sexual Orientation Says the 7th Circuit," *National Law Review*, April 14, 2017, https://www.natlawreview .com/article/sex-discrimination-includes-sexual-orientation-says-7th-circuit.

32 Fred Fejes, *Gay Rights and Moral Panic: The Origins of America's Debate on Homosexuality* (New York: Palgrave, 2008).

33 "Gay Rights Incorporated in Very Unusual Manner," 3.

34 "Gay Rights Incorporated in Very Unusual Manner," 3.

35 Marjorie Rowland, interview with author, July 28, 2016.

36 "Opinion of the Trial Court," U.S. District Court for the Southern District of Ohio, Western Division, case no. C-3-75-125, p. 12.

37 "Opinion of the Trial Court," pp. 3–4.

38 "Opinion of the Trial Court," p. 4.

39 "Special Verdict Law and Legal Definition," USLegal.com, accessed September 19, 2017, https://definitions.uslegal.com/s/special-verdict/. See Joan Black, "*Rowland v. Mad River School District*: Counselor's Sexual Freedom Upheld," *Guild Notes* 11 (January/February 1982): 19; and Diane Wiley, "Expanding Civil Voir Dire," *Guild Notes* 11 (January/February 1982): 19, for a review of the voir dire strategy in Rowland's trial. Black was cocounsel with Sandy Spater for Rowland at the district trial.

40 Rowland v. Mad River Local School District, #76-2450, Sixth Circuit Court, 1977, summarized in "Opinion of the Trial Court," p. 24.

41 Rowland v. Mad River Local School District, #76-2450, Sixth Circuit Court, 1977, summarized in "Opinion of the Trial Court," p. 31.

42 Pickering v. Board of Education (1968), quoted in "Opinion of the Trial Court," pp. 5–6.

43 "Opinion of the Trial Court," p. 13.

44 "Opinion of the Trial Court," p. 12.

45 "Opinion of the Trial Court," p. 13.

46 "Bisexual Teacher Wins Suit," *Mansfield News-Journal*, October 23, 1981, 17.

47 Marjorie Rowland, interview with authors, June 20, 2017.

48 Marjorie Rowland, interview with authors, June 20, 2017.

49 Marjorie Rowland, interview with author, July 28, 2016.

50 "Bisexual Ms. Rowland Now Faces Food Stamp Charges," *Xenia Daily Gazette*, October 24, 1981, 1.

51 "Rowland Hearing Continued," *Xenia Daily Gazette*, October 29, 1981, 1.

52 "Bisexual Ms. Rowland Now Faces Food Stamp Charges," 1.

53 "Bisexual Ms. Rowland Now Faces Food Stamp Charges," 1.

54 "Rowland Hearing Continued," 1.

55 "Bisexual Ms. Rowland Now Faces Food Stamp Charges," 1.

56 "Schenck Seeks Daytonian to Defend His Office," *Xenia Daily Gazette*, December 12, 1981, 3.

57 "Bisexual Ms. Rowland Now Faces Food Stamp Charges," 1.

58 Mary McCarty, "Bill Schenck's M.O. as a Prosecutor: Part Bluff, Part Guts, Part Shrewd Instinct," *Dayton Daily News*, January 23, 1994, http://www.myday tondailynews.com/news/local-obituaries/from-the-archives-prosecuting-with -pizazz/wl6vi6K4Dd1RjIiw5zUrHI/.

59 McCarty, "Bill Schenck's M.O."

60 McCarty.

61 "Rowland Hearing Continued," 1.

62 Marjorie Rowland, interviews with authors, July 28, 2016, and June 20, 2017.

63 Diane Ryder, "Geauga Official Known for His Colorful Comments," *The News-Herald*, December 19, 2008, http://www.news-herald.com/article/HR /20081219/NEWS/312199961.

64 Ryder, "Geauga Official."

65 "Rowland Sentenced in Welfare Violation Case," *Xenia Daily Gazette*, December 21, 1985, 2.

66 Kristina Goetz, "Federal Judge from Louisville Dies," *Courier-Journal*, March 13, 2016, http://www.courier-journal.com/story/news/local/2016/03/13/federal-judge -louisville-dies/81739004/.

67 Arthur M. Kaufman, "Judge Robert B. Krupansky: A Personal Remembrance," *Inter Alia* (Winter 2005), http://www.fba-ndohio.org/Resources/Documents /Winter%202005.pdf.

68 Nathaniel R. Jones, *Answering the Call: An Autobiography of the Modern Struggle to End Racial Discrimination in America* (New York: New Press, 2016), 226.

69 Russell Kirk, "Corruption in Court," *Bluefield Daily Telegraph*, January 9, 1973, 4.

70 "George Clifton Edwards, Jr.," Revolvy, accessed September 25, 2017, https://www .revolvy.com/main/index.php?s=George%20Clifton%20Edwards,%20Jr.&item _type=topic. See also George Edwards, *Pioneer-at-Law: A Legacy in the Pursuit of Justice* (New York: Norton, 1974).

71 "Pioneer-at-Law: A Legacy in the Pursuit of Justice," *Kirkus Reviews*, September 23, 1974, https://www.kirkusreviews.com/book-reviews/george-edwards /pioneer-at-law-a-legacy-in-the-pursuit-of-justi/.

72 "Opinion of the United States Court of Appeals for the Sixth Circuit," case no. 82-3218, March 22, 1984, p. 9.

73 "Opinion of the United States Court of Appeals for the Sixth Circuit," pp. 13–14.

74 "Opinion of the United States Court of Appeals for the Sixth Circuit," p. 15.

75 "Opinion of the United States Court of Appeals for the Sixth Circuit," p. 15.

76 "Opinion of the United States Court of Appeals for the Sixth Circuit," p. 16.

77 "Opinion of the United States Court of Appeals for the Sixth Circuit," p. 17.

78 "Opinion of the United States Court of Appeals for the Sixth Circuit," p. 18.

79 "Opinion of the United States Court of Appeals for the Sixth Circuit," p. 19.

80 "Opinion of the United States Court of Appeals for the Sixth Circuit," p. 19.

81 "Opinion of the United States Court of Appeals for the Sixth Circuit," p. 15.

82 "Petition for Rehearing with a Suggestion for Rehearing En Banc Submitted by Plaintiff-Appellee Marjorie Rowland," U.S. Court of Appeals for the Sixth Circuit, No. 82-3218, p. 1.

83 "Petition for Rehearing," p. 13.

84 "Petition for Rehearing," p. 14; emphasis in original.

85 "Petition for Rehearing," p. 14.

86 "Petition for Rehearing," pp. 4–5.

87 "Petition for Rehearing," p. 5.

88 "Petition for Rehearing," p. 6.

89 "Xenian Dismissed from Dayton Police Force," *Xenia Daily Gazette*, March 24, 1984, 3.

90 "Gazette Beats," *Xenia Daily Gazette*, March 4, 1986, 5.

91 "ACLU Meeting Scheduled," *Xenia Daily Gazette*, June 22, 1985, 5.

92 Jon Henry, "Rowland Says YS Cops Refuse Assault Charges," *Xenia Daily Gazette*, July 25, 1985, 1.

93 "Domestic Violence Law Under YS Review," *Xenia Daily Gazette*, March 5, 1985, 3.

94 Henry, "Rowland Says," 1.

95 "Domestic Violence Arrests Is Topic of Antioch Friday Forum," *Xenia Daily Gazette*, October 1, 1985, 1.

96 "Board Certifies 149 November Candidates," *Xenia Daily Gazette*, August 28, 1985, 2.

97 "ACLU Meeting Is Wednesday," *Xenia Daily Gazette*, November 12, 1985, 2.

98 "Rowland Sentenced in Welfare Violation Case," *Xenia Daily Gazette*, December 21, 1985, 2.

99 Marjorie Rowland, interview with author, July 28, 2016.

100 Sample questions come from the current Character and Fitness Application, but the questions in 1986 were similar. "Sample Character and Fitness Application," Arizona Courts, accessed September 29, 2017, http://www.azcourts.gov/Portals /26/admis/pdf/SampleCharacterAndFitnessApplication.pdf.

101 Marjorie Rowland, interview with author, July 28, 2016.

102 Marjorie Rowland, interview with author, July 28, 2016.

Chapter 3   The Meaning of *Mad River*

Epigraph: Snetsinger v. Montana University System (Mont. 2004), Justice James C. Nelson dissent, pp. 27–28.

1 William N. Eskridge, Jr. and Nan D. Hunter, *Sexuality, Gender, and the Law*, 2nd ed. (New York: Foundation, 2004), 633.

2 Court Listener, accessed January 11, 2019, https://www.courtlistener.com/?q =%22Rowland+v.+Mad+River%22.

3 Wagner v. Genesee County Bd. Of Com'rs, 607 F. Supp. 1158 (E.D. Mich. 1985), p. 1169.

4 High Tech Gays v. Defense Indus. SEC. Clear. Off., 668 F. Supp. 1361 (N.D. Cal. 1987), p. 1369. Brennan quoting Plyler v. Doe, 457 U.S. 202, 216 n. 14, 102 S. Ct. 2382, 2394 n. 14, 72 L. Ed. 2d 786 (1982).

5 For a clear introduction to levels of scrutiny, see Mariam Morshedi, "Levels of Scrutiny," Subscript Law, accessed February 14, 2019, https://www.subscriptlaw .com/blog/levels-of-scrutiny.

6 Level of scrutiny analysis was not always of critical importance because some discriminatory laws could be found unconstitutional at the lowest level of rational basis review. See, for instance, District Judge Thelton Henderson's sweeping statement in *High Tech Gays v. Defense Indus. SEC. Clear. Off.*, 668 F. Supp. 1361 (N.D. Cal. 1987), p. 1373. The judge found "the undisputed facts show that defendants' actions violate plaintiffs' rights under the equal protection clause under strict scrutiny, heightened scrutiny, and rational basis scrutiny, because there is no rational basis for defendants' subjecting all gay applicants to expanded investigations and mandatory adjudications while not doing the same for all straight applicants. Defendants' treatment of lesbians and gay men reflects irrational prejudice and outmoded stereotypes and notions about lesbians and gay men, not rational considerations." Although the U.S. Supreme Court sidestepped the issue in *Windsor v. United States* and *Obergefell v. Hodges*, both the Second Circuit (in *Windsor*) and the Supreme Court of Connecticut (in *Kerrigan v. Commissioner of Public Health*) held that sexual minorities constitute a quasi-suspect class.

7 In *High Tech Gays v. Defense Indus. SEC. Clear. Off.* plaintiffs brought a nation-wide class action, challenging a Department of Defense policy that subjected lesbian and gay applicants for industrial security clearances to expanded investigations and mandatory adjudications because of their sexuality. District Judge Thelton E. Henderson granted plaintiffs' motions for summary judgment in respect to their equal protection and First Amendment claims.

8 When the U.S. Supreme Court struck down employment discrimination against LGBT workers in 2020, however, it based the decision on discrimination "because of sex," prohibited in Title VII of the 1964 Civil Rights Act.

9 Johnson v. Orr, 617 F. Supp. 170 (E.D. Cal. 1985), p. 171.

10 Johnson v. Orr, 617 F. Supp. 170 (E.D. Cal. 1985), p. 171.

11 Johnson v. Orr, 617 F. Supp. 170 (E.D. Cal. 1985), pp. 172–173.

12 The legal definition of *pure speech* refers to "communication of ideas through spoken or written words or through conduct limited in form to that necessary to convey the idea." See *Merriam-Webster Legal Dictionary*, s.v. "pure speech," accessed August 29, 2021, https://www.merriam-webster.com/legal/pure%20 speech. The First Amendment protects symbolic speech (ideas conveyed through actions and symbols) as well as the verbal expression of pure speech. Courts use the Spence test to determine whether specific expressive conduct is "'expressive' enough to warrant First Amendment protection." See David L. Hudson Jr., "Spence Test," First Amendment Encyclopedia, accessed August 29, 2021, https://www.mtsu.edu/first-amendment/article/1590/spence-test.

13 Johnson v. Orr, 617 F. Supp. 170 (E.D. Cal. 1985), p. 171.

14 Johnson v. Orr, 617 F. Supp. 170 (E.D. Cal. 1985), p. 175.

15 Johnson v. Orr, 617 F. Supp. 170 (E.D. Cal. 1985), p. 176.

16 Johnson v. Orr, 617 F. Supp. 170 (E.D. Cal. 1985), pp. 176–177.

17 BenShalom v. Marsh, 703 F. Supp. 1372 (D. Wis. 1989), p. 1373, quoting the regulation; Sergeant Perry Watkins v. United States Army, 875 F.2d 699 (9th Cir. 1989).

18 Sergeant Perry Watkins v. United States Army, 875 F.2d 699 (9th Cir. 1989).

19 In determining whether a person belongs to a suspect class, the group must be considered a discrete and insular minority. Courts consider a number of factors in making this determination, including but not limited to the following: (1) Is there a history of discrimination against the group? (2) Is the group politically power-less? (3) Does the group possess an immutable trait? (4) Is that trait relevant to the group's participation or ability to contribute to society? Courts need not tick off each of these elements to define a group as a suspect class; most often they consider the question comprehensively. Kenji Yoshino cites "pluralism anxiety" in explaining that the court has, for decades, resisted extending constitutional protections to new groups. See "Suspect Classification," Legal Information Institute, accessed December 16, 2020, https://www.law.cornell.edu/wex/suspect _classification; Eric Berger, "Same-Sex Marriage, Heightened Scrutiny and the Problem of 'Animus,'" Jurist, accessed December 15, 2020, https://www.jurist.org /commentary/2015/03/eric-berger-samesex-marriages/; Kenji Yoshino, "The New Equal Protection," *Harvard Law Review* 124 (2011): 747–803, http://harvardlaw review.org/wp-content/uploads/pdfs/vol124_yoshino.pdf.

20 Brennan quoted in Sergeant Perry Watkins v. United States Army, 875 F.2d 699 (9th Cir. 1989), Norris concurring.

21 Quoting from High Tech Gays v. Defense Indus. SEC. Clear. Off. in Sergeant
    Perry Watkins v. United States Army, 875 F.2d 699 (9th Cir. 1989), Norris
    concurring.

22 Sergeant Perry Watkins v. United States Army, 875 F.2d 699 (9th Cir. 1989),
    Norris concurring.

23 Sergeant Perry Watkins v. United States Army, 875 F.2d 699 (9th Cir. 1989),
    Norris concurring.

24 Brennan quoted in Sergeant Perry Watkins v. United States Army, 875 F.2d 699
    (9th Cir. 1989), Norris concurring.

25 David W. Dunlap, "Perry Watkins, 48, Gay Sergeant Won Court Battle with
    Army," *New York Times*, March 21, 1996, https://www.nytimes.com/1996/03/21
    /nyregion/perry-watkins-48-gay-sergeant-won-court-battle-with-army.html.

26 AR 140-111, table 4-2, cited in BenShalom v. Marsh, 703 F. Supp. 1372 (D. Wis.
    1989), p. 1374.

27 BenShalom v. Marsh, 703 F. Supp. 1372 (D. Wis. 1989), p. 1377.

28 BenShalom v. Marsh, 703 F. Supp. 1372 (D. Wis. 1989), pp. 1379–1380.

29 Cited in Able v. United States, 968 F. Supp. 850 (E.D.N.Y 1997), p. 852.

30 Brennan quoted in Able v. United States, 968 F. Supp. 850 (E.D.N.Y 1997),
    pp. 862–863.

31 Able v. United States, 968 F. Supp. 850 (E.D.N.Y 1997), p. 862.

32 Able v. United States, 968 F. Supp. 850 (E.D.N.Y 1997), p. 864.

33 Snetsinger v. Montana University Sy (Mont. 2004), Nelson concurring, p. 19.

34 Donaldson v. State of Montana, 2012 MT 288, p. 1.

35 Donaldson v. State of Montana, 2012 MT 288, p. 4.

36 Donaldson v. State of Montana, 2012 MT 288, Nelson dissent, p. 26. See Cary
    Griffith, "The Life and Career of James C. Nelson, Justice, Montana Supreme
    Court," Law Crossing, accessed January 18, 2019, https://www.lawcrossing.com
    /article/355/James-C-Nelson-Justice-Montana-Supreme-Court/. Nelson received
    the Montana Trial Lawyers Public Service Award, 2013; Montana American Civil
    Liberties Janette Rankin Award, 2013; and the American Bar Association
    Stonewall Award, 2014.

37 Donaldson v. State of Montana, 2012 MT 288, Nelson dissent, p. 27.

38 Donaldson v. State of Montana, 2012 MT 288, Nelson dissent, p. 130.

39 Dean v. District of Columbia, 653 A.2d 307 (D.C. 1995).

40 In Re Marriage Cases, 143 Cal. App. 4th 873 (Cal. Ct. App. 2006), p. 686. See also
    Andersen v. King County, 138 P.3d 963 (Wash. 2006).

41 Conaway v. Deane (Md. 2007), p. 607.

42 Kerrigan v. Commissioner of Public Health, p. 412. In this case, the court did not
    go so far as to recognize homosexuals as a suspect class.

43 Windsor v. United States (2d Cir. 2012), pp. 22–33.

44 Berger, "Same-Sex Marriage."

45 Altogether, six of the court cases that cited *Rowland v. Mad River* involved
    teachers, school districts, or university systems. Four of these, including the
    aforementioned *Snetsinger v. Montana University System*, cited the Sixth Circuit
    ruling. In addition to that case, in 1987 the New Mexico Court of Appeals upheld
    a trial court's dismissal of a case brought against the Carlsbad School District by
    parents who held the district responsible for a teacher's misconduct. The teacher
    allegedly obtained marijuana for students and assisted them in the use of it during

school time. The court dismissed charges against the district, in part, because there was "no allegation that defendant, by policy or custom, sanctioned the teacher's conduct." The court referred to *Rowland* in explaining why the local governing body could not be held liable under 42 U.S.C. Section 1983. The defendant might have been found responsible for unconstitutional actions set in place through custom or policy (a point established in *Rowland*), but it was not shown that the action in the New Mexico case represented official policy. In *Adkins v. Stow City School District Board of Education*, the Ohio Court of Appeals reversed a lower court ruling in favor of a high school teacher who lost his coaching job after the first losing season for the team in a nine-year run. The coach argued that his dismissal as coach violated the First Amendment free speech clause because he was fired following remarks he made to the *Akron Beacon Journal*. The court of appeals cited *Rowland* to explain that constitutionally protected speech must address matters of public concern, and it fixed the coach's statement within the realm of personal interest. The coach's claim was dismissed. In 1991 a district court in Ohio denied a school district's motion for summary judgment against a teacher who was challenging her dismissal on the basis of sex discrimination. The teacher claimed she was dismissed because she was an unwed mother who had recently given birth through the means of artificial insemination. A number of complaints were brought in the complex case with a single reference to *Rowland* appearing in the school district's argument that they had not treated the teacher differently from other similarly situated persons. The court rejected this reasoning. See Rubio v. Carlsbad Mun. School Dist. (N.M. Ct. App. 1987), p. 921; Adkins v. Stow City School Dist. Bd. of Edn. (Ohio Ct. App. 1990), pp. 536–537; and Cameron v. Bd. of Educ. of Hillsboro, Ohio Sch. D. (S.D. Ohio 1991), p. 237.

46 Vernon R. Jantz v. Cleofas F. Muci, Lambda Legal Defense and Education Fund, Inc. American Civil Liberties Union Foundation and American Civil Liberties Union of Kansas National Conference of Gay and Lesbian Elected Officials, Amici Curiae, 976 F.2d 623 (10th Cir. 1992), p. 14.

47 Letter drafted by Mosher, signed by Mosher and Kimball, reviewed by Poulsen, quoted in Weaver v. Nebo School Dist. (D. Utah 1998), pp. 1281–1282.

48 Letter signed by Mosher and Kimball, quoted in *Weaver v. Nebo School Dist.* (D. Utah 1998), p. 1282.

49 Weaver v. Nebo School Dist., p. 1284.

50 Weaver v. Nebo School Dist., p. 1284.

51 Weaver v. Nebo School Dist., p. 1290.

52 Weaver v. Nebo School Dist., p. 1289.

53 Miller v. Weaver, UT 12, 66 P.3d 592 (2003), p. 600.

54 Rowland v. Mad River Local School Dist., Montgomery County, Ohio, 470 U.S. 1009 (1985), p. 1018.

55 Sergeant Perry Watkins v. United States Army, 875 F.2d 699 (9th Cir. 1989), Norris concurring.

56 Kenji Yoshino, *Covering: The Hidden Assault on our Civil Rights* (New York: Random House, 2006), 70.

57 Cited in Able v. United States, 968 F. Supp. 850 (E.D.N.Y 1997), p. 852.

58 See Karen Graves, "'A Matter of Public Concern': The First Amendment and Equal Employment for LGBT Educators," *History of Education Quarterly* 58, no. 3 (August 2018): 453–460, https://doi.org/10.1017/heq.2018.23.

59 Until the 2020 Supreme Court decision *Bostock v. Clayton County*, only twenty-one states and the District of Columbia prohibited employment discrimination based on sexual orientation and gender identity. An additional eight states prohibited discrimination based on sexual orientation and gender identity for public employees, and four more prohibited discrimination against public employees on the basis of sexual orientation only. Educators in seventeen states remained unprotected from employment discrimination on the basis of sexual orientation and gender identity. See "State Maps of Laws & Policies: Employment," Human Rights Campaign, accessed February 16, 2019, https://www.hrc.org/state-maps/employment.

60 Ruthann Robson, *Gay Men, Lesbians, and the Law* (New York: Chelsea House, 1997), 53.

61 William N. Eskridge Jr., *Gaylaw: Challenging the Apartheid of the Closet* (Cambridge, MA: Harvard University Press, 1999), 181.

62 Eskridge, *Gaylaw*, 180.

63 Weaver v. Nebo School Dist., p. 1291.

64 Cheshire Calhoun, *Feminism, the Family, and the Politics of the Closet: Lesbian and Gay Displacement* (Oxford: Oxford University Press, 2000), 93.

65 Calhoun, *Feminism*, 94–95.

66 Calhoun, 94.

67 Paul Siegel, "Lesbian and Gay Rights as a Free Speech Issue," *Journal of Homosexuality* 21, nos. 1–2 (1991): 251, https://doi.org/10.1300/J082v21n01_14. See also Rhonda R. Rivera, "Queer Law: Sexual Orientation Law in the Mid-Eighties Part I," *University of Dayton Law Review* 10, no. 3 (1985): 500. When the Supreme Court finally ruled on LGBT employment discrimination in 2020, opposing counsel abandoned the constitutional claims altogether. The court weighed the question in light of the more narrowly focused definition of sex in Title VII of the Civil Rights Act of 1964, which prohibits workplace discrimination on the basis of race, color, religion, sex, or national origin.

68 Judith Butler, "The Criminalization of Knowledge," *Chronicle of Higher Education*, May 27, 2018, https://www.chronicle.com/article/The-Criminalization-of/243501.

69 Butler, "Criminalization of Knowledge."

Chapter 4   "Coming Out of the Classroom Closet"

Epigraph: Shanna Peeples, quoted in Madeline Will, "LGBTQ Teachers Await Decision on Discrimination Protections," *Education Week* 39, no. 18 (January 14, 2020), https://www.edweek.org/policy-politics/lgbtq-teachers-await-decision-on-discrimination-protections/2020/01.

1 Steven V. Roberts, "The Nation; Reagan's Social Issues Gone but Not Forgotten," *New York Times*, September 11, 1988, https://www.nytimes.com/1988/09/11/weekinreview/the-nation-reagan-s-social-issues-gone-but-not-forgotten.html.

2 Mike Hammer, "Teacher Firings Allowed: Bill Hits Homosexuals," *Daily Oklahoman*, February 8, 1978; quoted in Clifford J. Rosky, "Anti-Gay Curriculum Laws," *Utah Law Faculty Scholarship* 13 (2017): 18, https://dc.law.utah.edu/cgi/viewcontent.cgi?article=1012&context=scholarship.

3 The U.S. Court of Appeals for the Tenth Circuit noted, "On appeal NGTF contends that the statute violates plaintiff's members' rights to privacy and equal

protection, that it is void for vagueness, that it violates the Establishment Clause, and, finally, that it is overbroad." See National Gay Task Force (NGTF) v. Board of Education of the City of Oklahoma City, 729 F. 2d 1270 (1984), https://law .resource.org/pub/us/case/reporter/F2/729/729.F2d.1270.82-1912.html. See also Catherine Connell, *School's Out: Gay and Lesbian Teachers in the Classroom* (Oakland: University of California Press, 2015).

4 See Karen Graves, "Sexuality," in *Miseducation: A History of Ignorance-Making in America and Abroad*, ed. A. J. Angulo (Baltimore: Johns Hopkins University Press, 2016), 17–21; and Karen Graves, "A Matter of Public Concern: The First Amendment and Equal Employment for LGBT Educators," *History of Education Quarterly* 58, no. 3 (August 2018): 453–460.

5 Marc Fajer, "*Bowers v. Hardwick, Romer v. Evans*, and the Meaning of Anti-Discrimination Legislation," *National Journal of Sexual Orientation Law* 2, no. 1 (1996): 208–215. Justice Powell played a pivotal role in both *NGTF v. Board of Education* and *Bowers v. Hardwick*. His absence resulted in a 4–4 tie in *NGTF v. Board of Education* and left the Tenth Circuit Court's ruling to stand. Powell cast the deciding vote in *Bowers v. Hardwick*, noting later, "I think I probably made a mistake in that one." Quoted in John C. Jeffries Jr., *Justice Lewis F. Powell, Jr.* (New York: Charles Scribner's Sons, 1994), 530. For further analysis on this point, see Karen Graves, "Pivotal in His Absence: Lewis Powell's Influence on the Legal Status of Lesbian and Gay Teachers in America" (unpublished paper, presented at the International Standing Conference for the History of Education, London, 2014).

6 Christopher R. Leslie, "Creating Criminals: The Injuries Inflicted by Unenforced Sodomy Laws," *Harvard Civil Rights–Civil Liberties Law Review* 35 (2003): 112.

7 Leslie, "Creating Criminals," 114.

8 Justice Marshall quoted in Catherine A. Lugg, "Thinking about Sodomy: Public Schools, Legal Panopticons, and Queers," *Educational Policy* 20, no. 1 (January and March 2006): 35.

9 The examples of LGBTQ educators who fought for equal employment rights that we discuss throughout this book are not exhaustive.

10 Arthur Lipkin, "Wanda and the Wastebasket," in *One Teacher in 10: Gay and Lesbian Educators Tell Their Stories*, ed. Kevin Jennings (Boston: Alyson, 1994), 46.

11 Jill Terreri Ramos, "Twenty-Five Years Ago: A Key Moment in Gay Rights Fight," *Boston Globe*, November 21, 2014, https://www.bostonglobe.com/metro/2014/11 /20/twenty-five-years-ago-key-moment-gay-rights-fight /I7MuYr7NDw4okf4gOoyi8L/story.html.

12 Gary Campbell, "Coming Out of the Cloakroom," in *One Teacher in 10: Gay and Lesbian Educators Tell Their Stories*, ed. Kevin Jennings (Boston: Alyson, 1994), 136. Los Angeles was among the cities where lesbian, gay, and bisexual teachers first organized to fight employment discrimination, aligning their efforts with the national teachers' unions. Early local organizing activity also occurred in Boston, Baltimore, Chicago, Denver, Portland, San Francisco, and New York. See Jason Mayernick, "LGB Teacher Organizations from 1970–1985" (PhD diss., University of Maryland, College Park, 2019), 106.

13 Campbell, "Coming Out," 136.

14 Bob Baker, "2 Dozen Teachers, Staff Declare that They Are Gay," *Los Angeles Times*, October 12, 1991, http://articles.latimes.com/1991-10-12/news/mn-203_1 _los-angeles-school.

15 John P. Pikala, "The Life beyond the Vita," in *One Teacher in 10: Gay and Lesbian Educators Tell Their Stories*, ed. Kevin Jennings (Boston: Alyson, 1994), 89–90.

16 Pikala, "Life beyond the Vita," 90.

17 Pikala, 93.

18 Dan Steadman, dir., *Taboo Teaching: A Profile of Missouri Teacher Rodney Wilson* (**Los Angeles:** Circa 87 Films, 2019), accessed 18 January 2021, https://youtu.be /sNW4CBpj8HY; "About LGBT History Month," LGBT History Month, accessed January 18, 2021, https://lgbthistorymonth.com/background.

19 Ruth Irwin, "You Can't Tell Him I'm Not," in *One Teacher in 10: Gay and Lesbian Educators Tell Their Stories*, ed. Kevin Jennings (Boston: Alyson Publications, 1994), 102.

20 Irwin, "You Can't Tell Him," 103.

21 Irwin, 103–104.

22 Irwin, 104.

23 Rita M. Kissen, *The Last Closet: The Real Lives of Lesbian and Gay Teachers* (Portsmouth, NH: Heinemann, 1996), 87.

24 Scott Harris and George Ramos, "Gay Activists Vent Rage over Wilson's Veto; Protest; Governor's Rejection of Job Discrimination Bill Sparks Violence," *Los Angeles Times*, October 1, 1991, http://articles.latimes.com/1991-10-01/news/mn -3522_1_los-angeles-and-san-francisco; Daniel M. Weintraub and Scott Harris, "Gay Rights Protest Disrupts Wilson Speech," *Los Angeles Times*, October 2, 1991, http://articles.latimes.com/1991-10-02/news/mn-2872_1_gay-rights.

25 See William N. Eskridge Jr., *Gaylaw: Challenging the Apartheid of the Closet* (Cambridge, MA: Harvard University Press, 1999), 356–361; and Jerome Hunt, "A State-by-State Examination of Nondiscrimination Laws and Policies: State Nondiscrimination Policies Fill the Void but Federal Protections Are Still Needed," Center for American Progress Action Fund, June 2012, 3–4, accessed December 15, 2019, https://www.americanprogress.org/wp-content/uploads /issues/2012/06/pdf/state_nondiscrimination.pdf. Before the 2020 Supreme Court ruling in *Bostock v. Clayton County*, the Human Rights Campaign reported twenty-one states and the District of Columbia prohibited employment discrimination on the basis of sexual orientation and gender identity, one state prohibited employment discrimination on the basis of sexual orientation, seven states prohibited employment discrimination on the basis of sexual orientation and gender identity for public employees, and four states prohibited employment discrimination on the basis of sexual orientation for public employees. Seventeen states had no laws prohibiting employment discrimination on the basis of sexual orientation or gender identity. See "State Maps of Laws and Policies: Employment," Human Rights Campaign, accessed December 15, 2019, https://www.hrc .org/state-maps/employment.

26 Gay and Lesbian Archives of the Pacific Northwest, "The Story of Oregon's 1992 Measure 9," *GLAPN Newsletter*, November 2012, accessed September 12, 2018, https://www.glapn.org/6010Measure9Background.html.

27 Gay and Lesbian Archives of the Pacific Northwest, "Measure 9."

28 Stu Wasserman, "Oregon, in First, Votes by Mail on Anti-Gay Issue," *Los Angeles Times*, June 29, 1993, http://articles.latimes.com/1993-06-29/news/mn-8375_1 _oregon-gays.

29 David Foster, "Gay Rights and Religious Right on Collision Course on Idaho's Plains," *Los Angeles Times*, October 30, 1994, http://articles.latimes.com/1994-10 -30/news/mn-56459_1_gay-rights.

30 David W. Dunlap, "After Bitter Debate on Gay Rights, Maine Will Vote in Referendum on Discrimination," *New York Times*, November 5, 1995, https://www.nytimes.com/1995/11/05/us/after-bitter-debate-on-gay-rights -maine-will-vote-in-referendum-ondiscrimination.html; Kissen, *Last Closet*, 111.

31 Stephen Zamansky, "Colorado's Amendment 2 and Homosexuals' Right to Equal Protection of the Law," *Boston College Law Review* 35, no. 1 (1993), https:// lawdigitalcommons.bc.edu/cgi/viewcontent.cgi?referer=https://www.google.com /&httpsredir=1&article=1986&context=bclr.

32 Catherine A. Lugg, *U.S. Public Schools and the Politics of Queer Erasure* (New York: Palgrave, 2016), 55.

33 Zamansky, "Colorado's Amendment 2," 222.

34 "*Romer v. Evans*," Lambda Legal, accessed September 12, 2018, https://www .lambdalegal.org/in-court/cases/romer-v-evans.

35 Romer v. Evans, 517 U.S. 620 (1996).

36 "State Religious Freedom Restoration Acts," National Conference of State Legislatures, May 4, 2017, http://www.ncsl.org/research/civil-and-criminal-justice /state-rfra-statutes.aspx.

37 Kissen, *Last Closet*, 111.

38 Kissen, 115–116.

39 Kissen, ch. 9. One can draw parallels between the antigay campaigns of the 1990s and earlier attempts to oust gay and lesbian teachers, in terms of tactics and the impact on teachers. During the Johns Committee purge in Florida, for example, one school official reported that his county office intensified their scrutiny of job applications submitted by single male educators. See Karen L. Graves, *And They Were Wonderful Teachers: Florida's Purge of Gay and Lesbian Teachers* (Urbana: University of Illinois Press, 2009), 83.

40 Kissen, *Last Closet*, 74.

41 Kissen, 75.

42 Kissen, 101–103. See also Catherine A. Lugg, "Our Straight-laced Administrators: LGBT School Administrators, the Law, and the Assimilationist Imperative," *Journal of School Leadership* 13, no. 1 (2003): 51–85.

43 Eskridge, *Gaylaw*, 359.

44 Glover v. Williamsburg Local School District Board of Education, 20 F. Supp. 2d 1160 (S.D. Ohio 19989), May 18, 1998, https://law.justia.com/cases/federal/district -courts/FSupp2/20/1160/2423431/

45 Glover v. Williamsburg Local School District Board of Education, 20 F. Supp. 2d 1160 (S.D. Ohio 19989), May 18, 1998, https://law.justia.com/cases/federal/district -courts/FSupp2/20/1160/2423431/.

46 "LGBT Employment Discrimination in the United States," Wikipedia, accessed February 22, 2021, https://en.wikipedia.org/wiki/LGBT_employment _discrimination_in_the_United_States#Chronological_order.

47 Kristen V. Luschen and Lesley Bogad, "Bodies that Matter: Transgenderism, Innocence, and the Politics of 'Unprofessional' Pedagogy," *Sex Education* 3, no. 2 (2003): 148–149.

48 ABC *20/20*, quoted in Sheila L. Cavanagh, "Teacher Transsexuality: The Illusion of Sexual Difference and the Idea of Adolescent Trauma in the Dana Rivers Case," *Sexualities* 6, nos. 3–4 (2003): 362.

49 Connell, *School's Out*, 52.

50 Stuart Biegel, *The Right to Be Out: Sexual Orientation and Gender Identity in America's Public Schools* (Minneapolis: University of Minnesota Press, 2010), 68.

51 Biegel, *Right to Be Out*, 69.

52 Mark Walsh, "High Court Declines Case on Harassment of Gay Teacher," *Education Week* 22, no. 9 (October 30, 2002): 28.

53 Walsh, "High Court Declines," 28.

54 Biegel, *Right to Be Out*, 70.

55 Biegel, 10–12; "*Nabozny v. Podlesny*," Lambda Legal, accessed September 4, 2018, https://www.lambdalegal.org/in-court/cases/nabozny-v-podlesny.

56 Quoted in Biegel, *Right to Be Out*, 73.

57 Biegel, 12.

58 Supreme Court of the United States, Lawrence et al. v. Texas, Certiorari to the Court of Appeals of Texas, Fourteenth District, June 2003, accessed September 10, 2018, https://www.law.cornell.edu/supct/html/02-102.ZS.html.

59 Lawrence v. Texas, 539 U.S. 558 (2003). Justice Anthony Kennedy's role as author of majority opinions on the most critical civil rights cases for LGBT people to reach the U.S. Supreme Court is widely acknowledged. One commentator, reflecting on the decisions in *Romer v. Evans*, *Lawrence v. Texas*, *United States v. Windsor*, and *Obergefell v. Hodges*, described Kennedy as the "linchpin of the transformation of civil rights for the LGBTQ community." See Paul Smith, "Justice Kennedy: The Linchpin of the Transformation of Civil Rights for the LGBTQ Community," *SCOTUSblog*, June 28, 2018, https://www.scotusblog.com/2018/06/justice-kennedy-the-linchpin-of-the-transformation-of-civil-rights-for-the-lgbtq-community/. Also see Brent Kendall and Jess Bravin, "Justice Anthony Kennedy Defined His Career at Center of Biggest Decisions," *Wall Street Journal*, June 27, 2018, https://www.wsj.com/articles/supreme-court-justice-anthony-kennedy-announces-retirement-1530122570.

60 See Catherine Lugg's analysis on the ways in which legal status remained fragile for LGBT people in the years following the *Lawrence* decision. Lugg, "Thinking about Sodomy," 36.

61 David Stout, "Bush Backs Ban in Constitution on Gay Marriage," *New York Times*, February 24, 2004, https://www.nytimes.com/2004/02/24/politics/bush-backs-ban-in-constitution-on-gay-marriage.html.

62 Timothy J. Burger, "Inside George W. Bush's Closet," *Politico*, July/August 2014, https://www.politico.com/magazine/story/2014/06/inside-george-w-bushs-closet-108016_full.html.

63 "The Triumph of the Religious Right," *The Economist*, November 11, 2004, https://www.economist.com/special-report/2004/11/11/the-triumph-of-the-religious-right.

64 Connell, *School's Out*.

65 Complaint for Damages, Injunctive and Declaratory Relief, Frost v. Hesperia Unified School District, November 19, 2013, accessed September 10, 2018, https://www.lambdalegal.org/in-court/legal-docs/frost_ca_20131119_complaint.

66   Rick Rojas, "Hesperia Teacher Says She Was Fired for Being a Lesbian, Files Suit,"
     Los Angeles Times, November 19, 2013, http://articles.latimes.com/2013/nov/19
     /local/la-me-ln-hesperia-teacher-lesbian-harassment-suit-20131119.

67   Brett Bigham, "You Can Be Teacher of the Year and Still Get Fired for Being
     Gay," *Education Post*, October 2, 2017, http://educationpost.org/you-can-be
     -teacher-of-the-year-and-still-get-fired-for-being-gay/.

68   Carrie Maxwell, "Award-Winning Teacher Talks Settlement, White House Visit,"
     Windy City Times, July 5, 2016, http://www.windycitymediagroup.com/lgbt
     /Award-winning-teacher-talks-settlement-White-House-visit/55762.html.

69   Amanda Machado, "The Plight of Being a Gay Teacher: LGBT Educators Walk a
     Fine Line between Keeping Their Jobs and Being Honest with Their Students,"
     The Atlantic, December 16, 2014, https://www.theatlantic.com/education/archive
     /2014/12/the-plight-of-being-a-lgbt-teacher/383619/.

70   Kissen, *Last Closet*, 56.

71   Connell, *School's Out*, 32.

72   Myrna Olson, "A Study of Gay and Lesbian Teachers," *Journal of Homosexuality*
     13, no. 4 (1987): 73–80.

73   Meredith Bennett-Smith, "Carla Hale, Gay Teacher, Fired from Catholic High
     School after Being 'Outed' by Mother's Obituary," *Huffington Post*, April 18, 2013,
     https://www.huffingtonpost.com/2013/04/18/carla-hale-gay-fired-teacher-catholic
     -high-school_n_3103853.html.

74   Adam Ragusea, "Gay Teacher Files Sex Discrimination Claim against Georgia
     School," NPR, July 9, 2014, https://www.npr.org/2014/07/09/329235789/gay
     -teacher-files-sex-discrimination-claim-against-georgia-school.

75   Bennett-Smith, "Carla Hale, Gay Teacher."

76   Quoted in Margaret Renkl, "How to Defy the Catholic Church," *New York
     Times*, July 1, 2019, https://www.nytimes.com/2019/07/01/opinion/how-to-defy
     -the-catholic-church.html. See also Bennett-Smith.

Chapter 5   Movements Forward and Back

Epigraph: Marjorie Rowland, interview with author, July 28, 2016.

1   In his opinion, Justice Gorsuch left open the possibility that Title VII protections
     may be superseded by religious liberty claims under the free exercise clause of the
     First Amendment or the 1993 Religious Freedom Restoration Act. See Amanda
     Hollis-Brusky, "The Supreme Court Closed the Door on LGBTQ Employment
     Discrimination. But It Opened a Window," *Washington Post*, June 16, 2020,
     https://www.washingtonpost.com/politics/2020/06/16/supreme-court-closed
     -door-lgbtq-employment-discrimination-it-opened-window/.

2   William J. Hall and Mimi V. Chapman, "Fidelity of Implementation of a State
     Anti-Bullying Policy with a Focus on Protected Social Classes," *Journal of School
     Violence* 17, no. 1 (2018): 58–73; William J. Hall and Mimi V. Chapman, "The Role
     of School Context in Implementing a Statewide Anti-Bullying Policy and
     Protecting Students," *Educational Policy* 32, no. 4 (2018): 507–539.

3   Movement Advancement Project and GLSEN, *Separation and Stigma: Transgen-
     der Youth and School Facilities* (Boulder, CO: MAP, 2017), 6.

4   Erica L. Green, Katie Benner, and Robert Pear, "'Transgender' Could Be Defined Out of Existence under Trump Administration," *New York Times*, October 21, 2018, https://www.nytimes.com/2018/10/21/us/politics/transgender-trump -administration-sex-definition.html.

5   Ashley P. Taylor, "Trump Administration's Definitions of Sex Defy Science," *The Scientist*, October 23, 2018, https://www.the-scientist.com/news-opinion/trump -administrations-definitions-of-sex-defy-science—64993.

6   Cited in Susan Miller, "Young Show Less LGBTQ Tolerance," *USA Today*, June 27, 2019, 6A; Ginia Bellafante, "'Everybody Ain't Surfing This Rainbow Wave': Why Divisions Endure in Gay Rights," *New York Times*, June 28, 2019, https://www.nytimes.com/2019/06/28/nyregion/class-divisions-gay-rights-pride .html.

7   Miller, "Young Show Less," 1, 6A.

8   "National School Climate Survey Released," GLSEN, accessed March 3, 2019, https://www.glsen.org/article/glsen-releases-new-national-school-climate-survey -report. See full report at https://www.glsen.org/article/2017-national-school -climate-survey-1.

9   Catherine A. Lugg, "Sissies, Faggots, Lezzies, and Dykes: Gender, Sexual Orientation, and a New Politics of Education?," *Educational Administration Quarterly* 39, no. 1 (February 2003): 124.

10 Jasmina Sinanovic, "Futures of the Field," CLAGS Center for LGBTQ Studies, March 1, 2013, https://clags.org/articles/futures-of-the-field/. An online College Board search revealed eighteen institutions offering an undergraduate major in gay and lesbian studies. See "Big Future College Search," College Board, accessed March 3, 2019, https://bigfuture.collegeboard.org/college-search?major=166 _Gay%20and%20Lesbian%20Studies.

11 Frank O. Dykes and John L. Delport, "Our Voices Count: The Lived Experiences of LGBTQ Educators and Its Impact on Teacher Education Preparation Pro- grams," *Teacher Education* 29, no. 2 (2018): 135.

12 Paul C. Gorski, Shannon N. Davis, and Abigail Reiter, "An Examination of the (In)visibility of Sexual Orientation, Heterosexism, Homophobia, and Other LGBTQ Concerns in U.S. Multicultural Teacher Education Coursework," *Journal of LGBT Youth* 10, no. 3 (2013): 224–248.

13 Elizabeth C. Payne and Melissa J. Smith, "Refusing Relevance: School Adminis- trator Resistance to Offering Professional Development Addressing LGBTQ Issues in Schools," *Educational Administration Quarterly* 54, no. 2 (April, 2018): 183–215.

14 John Ferrannini, "Newsome Signs LGBT Teacher Training Bill," *Bay Area Reporter*, October 15, 2019, https://www.ebar.com/news/latest_news//283137; Greg Burt, "Teeth Removed from Bill to Force LGBT Training on Teachers," California Family Council, September 10, 2019, https://californiafamily.org/2019 /teeth-removed-from-bill-to-force-lgbt-training-on-teachers/; Jeff Johnston, "Good News: California Backs Away from Mandatory LGBT Teacher Training," Daily Citizen, September 23, 2019, https://dailycitizen.focusonthefamily.com /good-news-california-backs-away-from-mandatory-lgbt-teacher-training/.

15 Melinda M. Mangin, "Transgender Students in Elementary Schools: How Supportive Principals Lead," *Educational Administration Quarterly* 56, no. 2 (April 2019): 1–34.

16 Michael P. O'Malley and Colleen A. Capper, "A Measure of the Quality of Educational Leadership Programs for Social Justice: Integrating LGBTIQ Identities into Principal Preparation," *Educational Administration Quarterly* 51, no. 2 (2015): 292.

17 Mollie Blackburn and C. J. Pascoe, "K-12 Students in Schools," in *LGBTQ Issues in Education: Advancing a Research Agenda*, ed. George L. Wimberly (Washington, DC: American Educational Research Association, 2015), 94; Joseph G. Kosciw, Emily A. Greytak, Adrian D. Zongrone, Caitlin M. Clark, and Nhan L. Truong, "The 2017 National School Climate Survey: The Experiences of Lesbian, Gay, Bisexual, Transgender, and Queer Youth in Our Nation's Schools," GLSEN, 2018, 56, accessed August 19, 2019, https://www.glsen.org/sites/default/files /GLSEN-2017-National-School-Climate-Survey-NSCS-Full-Report.pdf.

18 Steven Camicia and Juanjuan Zhu, "LGBTQ Inclusion and Exclusion in State Social Studies Standards," *Curriculum and Teaching Dialogue* 21, no. 1/2 (2019): 7–20.

19 Blackburn and Pascoe, "K-12 Students in Schools," 94–97, 99.

20 Sarah Schwartz, "Four States Now Require Schools to Teach LGBT History," *Education Week*, August 12, 2019, http://blogs.edweek.org/teachers/teaching _now/2019/08/four_states_now_require_schools_to_teach_lgbt_history.html; Harron Walker, "Here's Every State that Requires Schools to Teach LGBTQ+ History," Out, August 16, 2019, https://www.out.com/news/2019/8/16/heres -every-state-requires-schools-teach-lgbtq-history.

21 John Paul Brammer, "'No Promo Homo' Laws Affect Millions of Students across U.S.," NBC News, February 9, 2018, https://www.nbcnews.com/feature/nbc-out /no-promo-homo-laws-affect-millions-students-across-u-s-n845136. Legislative attacks on curriculum have expanded across the nation since this book has gone to press.

22 Casey Leins, "These States Require Schools to Teach LGBT History," *U.S. News and World Report*, August 14, 2019, https://www.usnews.com/news/best-states /articles/2019-08-14/states-that-require-schools-to-teach-lgbt-history.

23 See Karen Graves, "A Matter of Public Concern: The First Amendment and Equal Employment for LGBT Educators," *History of Education Quarterly* 58, no. 3 (August 2018): 460, https://doi.org/10.1017/heq.2018.23.

24 Jackie M. Blount, "School Workers," in *LGBTQ Issues in Education: Advancing a Research Agenda*, ed. George L. Wimberly (Washington, DC: American Educational Research Association, 2015), 161. See also Jackie M. Blount, *Fit to Teach: Same-Sex Desire, Gender, and School Work in the Twentieth Century* (Albany: State University of New York Press, 2005).

25 Blount, "School Workers," 161–162.

26 Jason Mayernick, "LGB Teacher Organizations from 1970–1985" (PhD diss., University of Maryland, College Park, 2019), 106.

27 Blount, "School Workers," 168; Mayernick, "LGB Teacher Organizations," 2–3, 260.

28 Blount, 168–170; Blount, *Fit to Teach*, 108–155; Karen Graves, "Political Pawns in an Educational Endgame: Reflections on Bryant, Briggs, and Some Twentieth-Century School Questions," *History of Education Quarterly* 53, no. 1 (February 2013): 1–20; Karen Harbeck, *Gay and Lesbian Educators: Personal Freedoms—Public Constraints* (Malden, MA: Amethyst, 1997), 37–98, 208–271;

Margaret A. Nash and Karen Graves, "Staking a Claim in Mad River: Advancing Civil Rights for Queer America," in *Principled Resistance: How Teachers Resolve Ethical Dilemmas*, ed. Doris A. Santoro and Lizabeth Cain (Cambridge, MA: Harvard Education Press, 2018), 171–185. See also Brad Sears, Nan D. Hunter, and Christy Mallory, "Documenting Discrimination on the Basis of Sexual Orientation and Gender Identity in State Employment," Williams Institute, September 2009, accessed August 14, 2019, https://williamsinstitute.law.ucla.edu /research/discrimination/documenting-discrimination-on-the-basis-of-sexual -orientation-and-gender-identity-in-state-employment/.

29 Catherine A. Lugg, "Thinking about Sodomy: Public Schools, Legal Panoptics, and Queers," *Educational Policy* 20 (2006): 35–58. See also Laurence H. Tribe, "*Lawrence v. Texas*: The 'Fundamental Right' that Dare Not Speak Its Name," *Harvard Law Review* 117, no. 6 (April 2004): 1893–1955.

30 Tribe, "*Lawrence v. Texas*," 1895.

31 See "Amici Briefs Filed with SCOTUS in LGBT Employment Discrimination Cases," Williams Institute, accessed August 14, 2019, https://williamsinstitute.law .ucla.edu/research/scotus-title-vii-amici/.

32 See Karen L. Graves, *And They Were Wonderful Teachers: Florida's Purge of Gay and Lesbian Teachers* (Urbana: University of Illinois Press, 2009), 125–140; Jonathan Zimmerman and Emily Robertson, *The Case for Contention: Teaching Controversial Issues in American Schools* (Chicago: University of Chicago Press, 2017).

33 James Baldwin, "A Talk to Teachers," in *James Baldwin: Collected Essays*, ed. Toni Morrison (New York: Library of America, 1998), 678–679.

34 Margaret A. Haley, "Why Teachers Should Organize," *Journal of Education* 60, no. 13 (September 29, 1904): 215, http://www.jstor.org/stable/44059391.

35 Blount, "School Workers," 161–162. See also Vanessa Siddle Walker, *The Lost Education of Horace Tate: Uncovering the Hidden Heroes Who Fought for Justice in Schools* (New York: New Press, 2018).

Bibliography

Court Cases

Able v. United States, 968 F. Supp. 850 (E.D.N.Y 1997).

Adkins v. Stow City School Dist. Bd. of Edn. (Ohio Ct. App. 1990).

Andersen v. King County, 138 P.3d 963 (Wash. 2006).

BenShalom v. Marsh, 703 F. Supp. 1372 (D. Wis. 1989).

Bostock v. Clayton County, 590 U.S. (2020).

Cameron v. Bd. of Educ. of Hillsboro, Ohio Sch. D. (S.D. Ohio 1991).

Complaint for Damages, Injunctive and Declaratory Relief, Frost v. Hesperia Unified School District, November 19, 2013. Accessed September 10, 2018. https://www.lambdalegal.org/in-court/legal-docs/frost_ca_20131119_complaint.

Conaway v. Deane (Md. 2007).

Court Listener. Landing page for search of terms "Rowland v. Mad River." Accessed January 11, 2019. https://www.courtlistener.com/?q=%22Rowland+v.+Mad+River%22.

Dean v. District of Columbia, 653 A.2d 307 (D.C. 1995).

Donaldson v. State of Montana, 2012 MT 288.

Glover v. Williamsburg Local School District Board of Education, 20 F. Supp. 2d 1160 (S.D. Ohio 19989), May 18, 1998.

High Tech Gays v. Defense Indus. SEC. Clear. Off., 668 F. Supp. 1361 (N.D. Cal. 1987).

In Re Marriage Cases, 143 Cal. App. 4th 873 (Cal. Ct. App. 2006).

Johnson v. Orr, 617 F. Supp. 170 (E.D. Cal. 1985).

Kerrigan v. Commissioner of Public Health, 289 Conn. 135, 957 A.2d 407.

Lawrence v. Texas, 539 US 558 (2003).

"Marjorie H. Rowland v. Mad River Local School District, Montgomery County, Ohio, 470 U.S. 1009 (1985)." Court Listener, n.d. https://www.courtlistener.com/opinion/111388/marjorie-h-rowland-v-mad-river-local-school-district-montgomery-county/.

Miller v. Weaver, UT 12, 66 P.3d 592 (2003).

Nabozny v. Podlesny, 92 F.3d 446.

"Nabozny v. Podlesny." Lambda Legal. Accessed September 4, 2018. https://www
.lambdalegal.org/in-court/cases/nabozny-v-podlesny.

National Gay Task Force v. Board of Education of the City of Oklahoma City, 729 F.
2d 1270 (1984).

"Opinion of the United States Court of Appeals for the Sixth Circuit," case
no. 82-3218, March 22, 1984.

"Opinion of the Trial Court," U.S. District Court for the Southern District of Ohio,
Western Division, case no. C-3-75-125.

"Petition for Rehearing with a Suggestion for Rehearing En Banc Submitted by
Plaintiff-Appellee Marjorie Rowland," U.S. Court of Appeals for the Sixth Circuit,
no. 82-3218.

Pickering v. Board of Education (1968), quoted in "Opinion of the Trial Court," U.S.
District Court for the Southern District of Ohio, Western Division, case no.
C-3-75-125, pp. 5–6.

Romer v. Evans, 517 U.S. 620 (1996).

Rowland v. Mad River Local School Dist., 470 U.S. 1009 (1985).

Rowland v. Mad River Local School District, #76-2450, Sixth Circuit Court, 1977,
summarized in "Opinion of the Trial Court," U.S. District Court for the Southern
District of Ohio, Western Division, case no. C-3-75-125.

Rubio v. Carlsbad Mun. School Dist. (N.M. Ct. App. 1987).

Sergeant Perry Watkins v. United States Army, 875 F.2d 699 (9th Cir. 1989).

Snetsinger v. Montana University Sy (Mont. 2004).

Supreme Court of the United States, Lawrence et al. v. Texas, Certiorari to the Court
of Appeals of Texas, Fourteenth District, June 2003. Accessed September 10, 2018.
https://www.law.cornell.edu/supct/html/02-102.ZS.html.

Vernon R. Jantz v. Cleofas F. Muci, Lambda Legal Defense and Education Fund, Inc.
American Civil Liberties Union Foundation and American Civil Liberties Union
of Kansas National Conference of Gay and Lesbian Elected Officials, Amici
Curiae, 976 F.2d 623 (10th Cir. 1992).

Wagner v. Genesee County Bd. Of Com'rs, 607 F. Supp. 1158 (E.D. Mich. 1985).

Weaver v. Nebo School Dist. (D. Utah 1998).

Wiemann v. Updegraff, 344 U.S. 183 (1952).

Windsor v. United States (2d Cir. 2012).

News Sources

"ACLU Meeting Is Wednesday." Xenia Daily Gazette, November 12, 1985.

"ACLU Meeting Scheduled." Xenia Daily Gazette, June 22, 1985.

Anapol, Avery. "DeVos Defends Controversial Guidance on Transgender Students."
The Hill, April 10, 2019. https://thehill.com/homenews/administration/438257
-dem-asks-devos-if-she-knew-of-potential-harm-to-transgender-students.

Baker, Bob. "2 Dozen Teachers, Staff Declare that They Are Gay." Los Angeles Times,
October 12, 1991. http://articles.latimes.com/1991-10-12/news/mn-203_1_los
-angeles-school.

Bellafante, Ginia. "'Everybody Ain't Surfing This Rainbow Wave': Why Divisions
Endure in Gay Rights." New York Times, June 28, 2019. https://www.nytimes.com
/2019/06/28/nyregion/class-divisions-gay-rights-pride.html.

Bennett-Smith, Meredith. "Carla Hale, Gay Teacher, Fired from Catholic High School after Being 'Outed' by Mother's Obituary." *Huffington Post*, April 18, 2013. https://www.huffingtonpost.com/2013/04/18/carla-hale-gay-fired-teacher-catholic -high-school_n_3103853.html.

"Bisexual Ms. Rowland Now Faces Food Stamp Charges." *Xenia Daily Gazette*, October 24, 1981.

"Bisexual Teacher Wins Suit." *Mansfield News-Journal*, October 23, 1981.

"Board Certifies 149 November Candidates." *Xenia Daily Gazette*, August 28, 1985.

Brammer, John Paul. "'No Promo Homo' Laws Affect Millions of Students across U.S." NBC News, February 9, 2018. Accessed November 13, 2019. https://www .nbcnews.com/feature/nbc-out/no-promo-homo-laws-affect-millions-students -across-u-s-n845136.

Broadwater, Luke, and Erica L. Green. "DeVos Vows to Withhold Desegregation Aid to Schools over Transgender Athletes." *New York Times*, September 18, 2020. https://www.nytimes.com/2020/09/18/us/transgender-students-betsy-devos.html.

Butler, Judith. "The Criminalization of Knowledge." *Chronicle of Higher Education*, May 27, 2018. https://www.chronicle.com/article/The-Criminalization-of/243501.

"Dayton, Ohio, Judge Voids a Busing Plan." *New York Times*, December 16, 1977. http://www.nytimes.com/1977/12/16/archives/dayton-ohio-judge-voids-a-busing -plan-says-naacp-failed-to-provide.html.

"Domestic Violence Arrests Is Topic of Antioch Friday Forum." *Xenia Daily Gazette*, October 1, 1985.

"Domestic Violence Law Under YS Review." *Xenia Daily Gazette*, March 5, 1985.

Dunlap, David W. "After Bitter Debate on Gay Rights, Maine Will Vote in Referendum on Discrimination." *New York Times*, November 5, 1995. https://www .nytimes.com/1995/11/05/us/after-bitter-debate-on-gay-rights-maine-will-vote-in -referendum-ondiscrimination.html.

———. "Perry Watkins, 48, Gay Sergeant Won Court Battle with Army." *New York Times*, March 21, 1996. https://www.nytimes.com/1996/03/21/nyregion/perry -watkins-48-gay-sergeant-won-court-battle-with-army.html.

Elsasser, Glen. "Supreme Court Keeping Silent in Cases Involving Gay Rights." *Chicago Tribune*, March 4, 1985. http://articles.chicagotribune.com/1985-03-04 /news/8501120683_1_supreme-court-justices-william-brennan-highest-court.

Ferrannini, John. "Newsome Signs LGBT Teacher Training Bill." *Bay Area Reporter*, October 15, 2019. https://www.ebar.com/news/latest_news//283137.

Foster, David. "Gay Rights and Religious Right on Collision Course on Idaho's Plains." *Los Angeles Times*, October 30, 1994. http://articles.latimes.com/1994-10 -30/news/mn-56459_1_gay-rights.

"Gay Rights Incorporated in Very Unusual Manner." *Mansfield News-Journal*, July 5, 1977.

"Gazette Beats." *Xenia Daily Gazette*, March 4, 1986.

Goetz, Kristina. "Federal Judge from Louisville Dies." *Courier-Journal*, March 13, 2016. http://www.courier-journal.com/story/news/local/2016/03/13/federal-judge -louisville-dies/81739004/.

Green, Erica L., Katie Benner, and Robert Pear. "'Transgender' Could Be Defined out of Existence under Trump Administration." *New York Times*, October 21, 2018. https://www.nytimes.com/2018/10/21/us/politics/transgender-trump -administration-sex-definition.html.

Greenhouse, Linda. "Supreme Court Roundup; Case Refused for Bisexual in Loss of
Job." *New York Times*, February 26, 1985. http://www.nytimes.com/1985/02/26/us
/supreme-court-roundup-case-refused-for-bisexual-in-los-of-job.html.

Hammer, Mike. "Teacher Firings Allowed: Bill Hits Homosexuals." *Daily Oklahoman*, February 8, 1978.

Harris, Scott, and George Ramos. "Gay Activists Vent Rage over Wilson's Veto;
Protest; Governor's Rejection of Job Discrimination Bill Sparks Violence." *Los
Angeles Times*, October 1, 1991. http://articles.latimes.com/1991-10-01/news/mn
-3522_1_los-angeles-and-san-francisco.

Henry, Jon. "Rowland Says YS Cops Refuse Assault Charges." *Xenia Daily Gazette*,
July 25, 1985.

Hollis-Brusky, Amanda. "The Supreme Court Closed the Door on LGBTQ Employment Discrimination. But It Opened a Window." *Washington Post*, June 16, 2020.
https://www.washingtonpost.com/politics/2020/06/16/supreme-court-closed-door
-lgbtq-employment-discrimination-it-opened-window/.

"Homosexual Counselor Loses Bid to Regain Job." *Xenia Daily Gazette*, August 23,
1977.

Johnston, Jeff. "Good News: California Backs Away from Mandatory LGBT
Teacher Training." Daily Citizen, September 23, 2019. https://dailycitizen
.focusonthefamily.com/good-news-california-backs-away-from-mandatory-lgbt
-teacher-training/.

Kendall, Brent, and Jess Bravin. "Justice Anthony Kennedy Defined His Career at
Center of Biggest Decisions." *Wall Street Journal*, June 27, 2018. https://www.wsj
.com/articles/supreme-court-justice-anthony-kennedy-announces-retirement
-1530122570.

Kirk, Russell. "Corruption in Court." *Bluefield Daily Telegraph*, January 9, 1973.

Leins, Casey. "These States Require Schools to Teach LGBT History." *U.S. News and
World Report*, August 14, 2019. https://www.usnews.com/news/best-states/articles
/2019-08-14/states-that-require-schools-to-teach-lgbt-history.

Maxwell, Carrie. "Award-Winning Teacher Talks Settlement, White House Visit."
Windy City Times, July 5, 2016. http://www.windycitymediagroup.com/lgbt
/Award-winning-teacher-talks-settlement-White-House-visit/55762.html.

McCarty, Mary. "Bill Schenck's M.O. as a Prosecutor: Part Bluff, Part Guts, Part
Shrewd Instinct." *Dayton Daily News*, January 23, 1994. http://www
.mydaytondailynews.com/news/local-obituaries/from-the-archives-prosecuting
-with-pizazz/wl6vi6K4Dd1RjIiw5zUrHI/.

Miller, Susan. "Young Show Less LGBTQ Tolerance." *USA Today*, June 27, 2019, 6A.

Millich, Gretchen. "East Lansing Marks 40th Anniversary of Gay Rights Ordinance."
WKAR, March 6, 2012. http://wkar.org/post/east-lansing-marks-40th
-anniversary-gay-rights-ordinance#stream/0.

Ragusea, Adam. "Gay Teacher Files Sex Discrimination Claim against Georgia
School." NPR, July 9, 2014. https://www.npr.org/2014/07/09/329235789/gay
-teacher-files-sex-discrimination-claim-against-georgia-school.

Ramos, Jill Terreri. "Twenty-Five Years Ago, a Key Moment in Gay Rights Fight."
Boston Globe, November 21, 2014. https://www.bostonglobe.com/metro/2014/11
/20/twenty-five-years-ago-key-moment-gay-rights-fight
/I7MuYr7NDw4okf4gOoyi8L/story.html.

Renkl, Margaret. "How to Defy the Catholic Church." *New York Times*, July 1, 2019. https://www.nytimes.com/2019/07/01/opinion/how-to-defy-the-catholic-church .html.

Roberts, Steven V. "The Nation; Reagan's Social Issues Gone but Not Forgotten." *New York Times*, September 11, 1988. https://www.nytimes.com/1988/09/11 /weekinreview/the-nation-reagan-s-social-issues-gone-but-not-forgotten.html.

Rojas, Rick. "Hesperia Teacher Says She Was Fired for Being a Lesbian, Files Suit." *Los Angeles Times*, November 19, 2013. http://articles.latimes.com/2013/nov/19 /local/la-me-ln-hesperia-teacher-lesbian-harassment-suit-20131119.

"Rowland Hearing Continued." *Xenia Daily Gazette*, October 29, 1981.

"Rowland Sentenced in Welfare Violation Case." *Xenia Daily Gazette*, December 21, 1985.

Ryder, Diane. "Geauga Official Known for His Colorful Comments." *The News-Herald*, December 19, 2008. http://www.news-herald.com/article/HR/20081219 /NEWS/312199961.

"Schenck Seeks Daytonian to Defend His Office." *Xenia Daily Gazette*, December 12, 1981.

Schwartz, Sarah. "Four States Now Require Schools to Teach LGBT History." *Education Week*, August 12, 2019. http://blogs.edweek.org/teachers/teaching_now /2019/08/four_states_now_require_schools_to_teach_lgbt_history.html.

Steele, Richard, and Holly Camp. "A 'No' to the Gays." *Newsweek*, June 20, 1977, 27. http://0-www.lexisnexis.com.dewey2.library.denison.edu/hottopics/lnacademic/.

Stout, David. "Bush Backs Ban in Constitution on Gay Marriage." *New York Times*, February 24, 2004. https://www.nytimes.com/2004/02/24/politics/bush-backs -ban-in-constitution-on-gay-marriage.html.

"Teacher Claims Ruling Ignored." *Xenia Daily Gazette*, March 8, 1975.

"Teacher Files New Suit Over Contract." *Xenia Daily Gazette*, June 3, 1975.

Walsh, Mark. "High Court Declines Case on Harassment of Gay Teacher." *Education Week* 22, no. 9 (October 30, 2002): 28.

Wasserman, Stu. "Oregon, in First, Votes by Mail on Anti-Gay Issue." *Los Angeles Times*, June 29, 1993. http://articles.latimes.com/1993-06-29/news/mn-8375_1 _oregon-gays.

Weintraub, Daniel M., and Scott Harris. "Gay Rights Protest Disrupts Wilson Speech." *Los Angeles Times*, October 2, 1991. http://articles.latimes.com/1991-10-02 /news/mn-2872_1_gay-rights.

Will, Madeline. "LGBTQ Teachers Await Decision on Discrimination Protections." *Education Week* 39, no. 18 (January 14, 2020). https://www.edweek.org/policy -politics/lgbtq-teachers-await-decision-on-discrimination-protections/2020/01.

"Xenian Dismissed from Dayton Police Force." *Xenia Daily Gazette*, March 24, 1984.

Zirin, Dave. "Betsy DeVos Attacks Trans Athletes Again." *The Nation*, October 23, 2020. https://www.thenation.com/article/society/trans-devos-title-ix/.

Other Sources

"About LGBT History Month." LGBT History Month. Accessed January 18, 2021. https://lgbthistorymonth.com/background.

"Amici Briefs Filed with SCOTUS in LGBT Employment Discrimination Cases." Williams Institute. Accessed August 14, 2019. https://williamsinstitute.law.ucla .edu/research/scotus-title-vii-amici/.

Bailey, Beth. *Sex in the Heartland*. Cambridge, MA: Harvard University Press, 2002.

Baldwin, James. "A Talk to Teachers." In *James Baldwin: Collected Essays*, edited by Toni Morrison, 678–686. New York: Library of America, 1998.

Berger, Eric. "Same-Sex Marriage, Heightened Scrutiny and the Problem of 'Animus.'" Jurist: Legal News and Commentary. Accessed December 15, 2020. https://www .jurist.org/commentary/2015/03/eric-berger-samesex-marriages/.

Biegel, Stuart. *The Right to Be Out: Sexual Orientation and Gender Identity in America's Public Schools*. Minneapolis: University of Minnesota Press, 2010.

"Big Future College Search." College Board. Accessed March 3, 2019. https:// bigfuture.collegeboard.org/college-search?major=166_Gay%20and%20Lesbian %20Studies.

Bigham, Brett. "You Can Be Teacher of the Year and Still Get Fired for Being Gay." *Education Post*, October 2, 2017. Accessed September 10, 2018. http:// educationpost.org/you-can-be-teacher-of-the-year-and-still-get-fired-for-being-gay/.

Black, Joan. "*Rowland v. Mad River School District*: Counselor's Sexual Freedom Upheld." *Guild Notes* 11 (January/February 1982): 19.

Blackburn, Mollie, and C. J. Pascoe. "K-12 Students in Schools." In *LGBTQ Issues in Education: Advancing a Research Agenda*, edited by George L. Wimberly, 89–104. Washington, DC: American Educational Research Association, 2015.

Blount, Jackie M. "School Workers." In *LGBTQ Issues in Education: Advancing a Research Agenda*, edited by George L. Wimberly, 161–173. Washington, DC: American Educational Research Association, 2015.

Blount, Jackie M. *Fit to Teach: Same-Sex Desire, Gender, and School Work in the Twentieth Century*. Albany: State University of New York Press, 2005.

Braukman, Stacy. *Communists and Perverts under the Palms: The Johns Committee in Florida, 1956–1965*. Gainesville: University Press of Florida, 2012.

Burger, Timothy J. "Inside George W. Bush's Closet." *Politico*, July/August 2014. https://www.politico.com/magazine/story/2014/06/inside-george-w-bushs-closet -108016_full.html.

Burt, Greg. "Teeth Removed from Bill to Force LGBT Training on Teachers." California Family Council, September 10, 2019. https://californiafamily.org/2019 /teeth-removed-from-bill-to-force-lgbt-training-on-teachers/

Calhoun, Cheshire. *Feminism, the Family, and the Politics of the Closet: Lesbian and Gay Displacement*. Oxford: Oxford University Press, 2000.

Camicia, Steven, and Juanjuan Zhu. "LGBTQ Inclusion and Exclusion in State Social Studies Standards." *Curriculum and Teaching Dialogue* 21, nos. 1–2 (2019): 7–20.

Campbell, Gary. "Coming Out of the Cloakroom." In *One Teacher in 10: Gay and Lesbian Educators Tell Their Stories*, edited by Kevin Jennings, 131–136. Boston: Alyson, 1994.

Cassanello, Robert, and Lisa Mills, dirs. *The Committee*. 2015; Orlando: University of Central Florida, 2016. DVD. https://www.pbs.org/show/committee/.

Cavanagh, Shelia L. "Teacher Transsexuality: The Illusion of Sexual Difference and the Idea of Adolescent Trauma in the Dana Rivers Case." *Sexualities* 6, nos. 3–4 (2003): 361–383.

Chiddester, Diane. *Two Hundred Years of Yellow Springs*. Yellow Springs, OH: Yellow Springs News, 2005.

Connell, Catherine. *School's Out: Gay and Lesbian Teachers in the Classroom.* Oakland: University of California Press, 2015.

"Dayton, OH." Atomic Heritage. Accessed September 6, 2017. http://www .atomicheritage.org/location/dayton-oh.

"Dayton, Ohio." City Data. Accessed September 6, 2017. http://www.city-data.com /city/Dayton-Ohio.html.

"Dayton, Ohio." Ohio History Central. Accessed September 6, 2017. http://www .ohiohistorycentral.org/w/Dayton,_Ohio.

Dykes, Frank O., and John L. Delport. "Our Voices Count: The Lived Experiences of LGBTQ Educators and Its Impact on Teacher Education Preparation Programs." *Teacher Education* 29, no. 2 (2018): 135–146.

Edwards, George. *Pioneer-at-Law: A Legacy in the Pursuit of Justice.* New York: Norton, 1974.

Eskridge, William N. *Gaylaw: Challenging the Apartheid of the Closet.* Cambridge, MA: Harvard University Press, 2009.

Eskridge, William N., Jr., and Nan D. Hunter. *Sexuality, Gender, and the Law.* 2nd ed. New York: Foundation, 2004.

Fajer, Marc. "*Bowers v. Hardwick, Romer v. Evans,* and the Meaning of Anti-Discrimination Legislation." *National Journal of Sexual Orientation Law* 2, no. 1 (1996): 208–215.

Fejes, Fred. *Gay Rights and Moral Panic: The Origins of America's Debate on Homosexuality.* New York: Palgrave Macmillan, 2008.

Gay and Lesbian Archives of the Pacific Northwest. "The Story of Oregon's 1992 Measure 9." *GLAPN Newsletter*, November 2012. Accessed September 12, 2018. https://www.glapn.org/6010Measure9Background.html.

"George Clifton Edwards, Jr." Revolvy. Accessed September 25, 2017. https://www.revolvy .com/main/index.php?s=George%20Clifton%20Edwards,%20Jr.&item_type=topic.

Gorski, Paul C., Shannon N. Davis, and Abigail Reiter. "An Examination of the (In)visibility of Sexual Orientation, Heterosexism, Homophobia, and Other LGBTQ Concerns in U.S. Multicultural Teacher Education Coursework." *Journal of LGBT Youth* 10, no. 3 (2013): 224–248.

Graves, Karen L. *And They Were Wonderful Teachers: Florida's Purge of Gay and Lesbian Teachers.* Urbana: University of Illinois Press, 2009.

———. "A Matter of Public Concern: The First Amendment and Equal Employment for LGBT Educators." *History of Education Quarterly* 58, no. 3 (August 2018): 453–460. https://doi.org/10.1017/heq.2018.23.

———. "Pivotal in His Absence: Lewis Powell's Influence on the Legal Status of Lesbian and Gay Teachers in America." Unpublished paper, presented at the International Standing Conference for the History of Education, London, 2014.

———. "Political Pawns in an Educational Endgame: Reflections on Bryant, Briggs, and Some Twentieth-Century School Questions." *History of Education Quarterly* 53, no. 1 (2013): 1–20.

———. "Sexuality." In *Miseducation: A History of Ignorance-Making in America and Abroad*, edited by A. J. Angulo, 53–72. Baltimore: Johns Hopkins University Press, 2016.

Griffith, Cary. "The Life and Career of James C. Nelson, Justice, Montana Supreme Court." Law Crossing. Accessed January 18, 2019. https://www.lawcrossing.com /article/355/James-C-Nelson-Justice-Montana-Supreme-Court/.

Haley, Margaret A. "Why Teachers Should Organize." *Journal of Education* 60, no. 13 (September 29, 1904): 215–216, 222. http://www.jstor.org/stable/44059391.

Hall, William J., and Mimi V. Chapman. "Fidelity of Implementation of a State Anti-Bullying Policy with a Focus on Protected Social Classes." *Journal of School Violence* 17, no. 1 (2018): 58–73.

Hall, William J., and Mimi V. Chapman. "The Role of School Context in Implementing a Statewide Anti-Bullying Policy and Protecting Students." *Educational Policy* 32, no. 4 (2018): 507–539.

Harbeck, Karen M. *Gay and Lesbian Educators: Personal Freedoms, Public Constraints*. Malden, MA: Amethyst, 1997.

Hudson, David L., Jr. "Spence Test." First Amendment Encyclopedia. Accessed August 29, 2021. https://www.mtsu.edu/first-amendment/article/1590/spence-test.

Hunt, Jerome. "A State-by-State Examination of Nondiscrimination Laws and Policies: State Nondiscrimination Policies Fill the Void but Federal Protections Are Still Needed." Center for American Progress Action Fund, June 2012. Accessed December 15, 2019. https://www.americanprogress.org/wp-content /uploads/issues/2012/06/pdf/state_nondiscrimination.pdf.

Irwin, Ruth. "You Can't Tell Him I'm Not." In *One Teacher in 10: Gay and Lesbian Educators Tell Their Stories*, edited by Kevin Jennings, 100–105. Boston: Alyson, 1994.

Jeffries, John C., Jr. *Justice Lewis F. Powell, Jr.* New York: Charles Scribner's Sons, 1994.

Johnson, David K. *The Lavender Scare: The Cold War Persecution of Gays and Lesbians in the Federal Government*. Chicago: University of Chicago Press, 2004.

Jones, Nathaniel R. *Answering the Call: An Autobiography of the Modern Struggle to End Racial Discrimination in America*. New York: New Press, 2016.

Kaufman, Arthur M. "Judge Robert B. Krupansky: A Personal Remembrance." *Inter Alia* (Winter 2005). http://www.fba-ndohio.org/Resources/Documents /Winter%202005.pdf.

Kinsey, Alfred, Wardell Pomeroy, and Clyde Martin. *Sexual Behavior in the Human Male*. Philadelphia: W. B. Saunders, 1948.

Kissen, Rita M. *The Last Closet: The Real Lives of Lesbian and Gay Teachers*. Portsmouth, NH: Heinemann, 1996.

Kosciw, Joseph G., Emily A. Greytak, Adrian D. Zongrone, Caitlin M. Clark, and Nhan L. Truong. "The 2017 National School Climate Survey: The Experiences of Lesbian, Gay, Bisexual, Transgender, and Queer Youth in Our Nation's Schools." GLSEN, 2018. Accessed August 19, 2019. https://www.glsen.org/sites/default/files /GLSEN-2017-National-School-Climate-Survey-NSCS-Full-Report.pdf.

Leslie, Christopher R. "Creating Criminals: The Injuries Inflicted by Unenforced Sodomy Laws." *Harvard Civil Rights–Civil Liberties Law Review* 35 (2003):103–181.

"LGBT Employment Discrimination in the United States." Wikipedia. Accessed February 22, 2021. https://en.wikipedia.org/wiki/LGBT_employment _discrimination_in_the_United_States#Chronological_order.

Lipkin, Arthur. "Wanda and the Wastebasket." In *One Teacher in 10: Gay and Lesbian Educators Tell Their Stories*, edited by Kevin Jennings, 39–49. Boston: Alyson Publications, 1994.

Lugg, Catherine A. "Our Straight-Laced Administrators: LGBT School Administrators, the Law, and the Assimilationist Imperative." *Journal of School Leadership* 13, no. 1 (2003): 51–85.

———. "Sissies, Faggots, Lezzies, and Dykes: Gender, Sexual Orientation, and a New Politics of Education?" *Educational Administration Quarterly* 39, no. 1 (February 2003): 95–134.

———. "Thinking about Sodomy: Public Schools, Legal Panopticons, and Queers." *Educational Policy* 20, no. 1 (January and March 2006): 35–58.

———. *U.S. Public Schools and the Politics of Queer Erasure.* New York: Palgrave, 2016.

Luschen, Kristen V., and Lesley Bogad. "Bodies that Matter: Transgenderism, Innocence, and the Politics of 'Unprofessional' Pedagogy." *Sex Education* 3, no. 2 (2003): 148–149.

Machado, Amanda. "The Plight of Being a Gay Teacher: LGBT Educators Walk a Fine Line between Keeping Their Jobs and Being Honest with Their Students." *The Atlantic*, December 16, 2014. https://www.theatlantic.com/education/archive/2014/12/the-plight-of-being-a-lgbt-teacher/383619/.

Mad River Local Schools. Homepage. Accessed September 6, 2017. https://www.madriverschools.org/.

Mangin, Melina M. "Transgender Students in Elementary Schools: How Supportive Principals Lead." *Educational Administration Quarterly* 15, NO. 2 (April 2019): 1–34.

Mayernick, Jason. "LGB Teacher Organizations from 1970–1985." PhD diss., University of Maryland, College Park, 2019.

Mirza, Shabab Ahmed, and Frank J. Bewkes. "Secretary DeVos Is Failing to Protect the Civil Rights of LGBTQ Students." *Center for American Progress*, July 29, 2019. https://www.americanprogress.org/issues/lgbtq-rights/reports/2019/07/29/472636/secretary-devos-failing-protect-civil-rights-lgbtq-students/.

Morshedi, Mariam. "Levels of Scrutiny." Subscript Law. Accessed February 14, 2019. https://www.subscriptlaw.com/blog/levels-of-scrutiny.

Movement Advancement Project and GLSEN. *Separation and Stigma: Transgender Youth and School Facilities.* Boulder: MAP, 2017.

Mueller, Robert. "Wright-Patterson Air Force Base." In *Air Force Bases, Vol. I: Active Air Force Bases Within the United States of America on 17 September 1982*, 596–610. Washington, DC: Office of Air Force History, 1989.

Murdoch, Joyce, and Deb Price. *Courting Justice: Gay Men and Lesbians v. the Supreme Court.* New York: Basic Books, 2001.

Nash, Margaret A., and Karen Graves. "Staking a Claim in Mad River: Advancing Civil Rights for Queer America." In *Principled Resistance: How Teachers Resolve Ethical Dilemmas*, edited by Doris A. Santoro and Lizabeth Cain, 171–185. Cambridge, MA: Harvard Education Press, 2018.

Nash, Margaret A., and Jennifer A. R. Silverman. "'An Indelible Mark': Gay Purges in Higher Education in the 1940s." *History of Education Quarterly* 55, no. 4 (November 2015): 441–459. https://doi.org/10.1111/hoeq.12135.

"National School Climate Survey Released." GLSEN. Accessed March 3, 2019. https://www.glsen.org/article/glsen-releases-new-national-school-climate-survey-report.

Olson, Myrna. "A Study of Gay and Lesbian Teachers." *Journal of Homosexuality* 13, no. 4 (1987): 73–80.

O'Malley, Michael P., and Colleen A. Capper. "A Measure of the Quality of Educational Leadership Programs for Social Justice: Integrating LGBTIQ Identities into Principal Preparation." *Educational Administration Quarterly* 51, no. 2 (2015): 290–330.

"Paul L. Dunbar." Ohio History Central. Accessed September 6, 2017. http://www.ohiohistorycentral.org/w/Paul_L._Dunbar.

Payne, Elizabeth C., and Melissa J. Smith. "Refusing Relevance: School Administrator Resistance to Offering Professional Development Addressing LGBTQ Issues in Schools." *Educational Administration Quarterly* 54, no. 2 (April 2018): 183–215.

Pikala, John P. "The Life beyond the Vita." In *One Teacher in 10: Gay and Lesbian Educators Tell Their Stories*, edited by Kevin Jennings, 86–94. Boston: Alyson, 1994.

"Pioneer-at-Law: A Legacy in the Pursuit of Justice." *Kirkus Reviews*, September 23, 1974. https://www.kirkusreviews.com/book-reviews/george-edwards/pioneer-at -law-a-legacy-in-the-pursuit-of-justi/.

Poucher, Judith. *State of Defiance: Challenging the Johns Committee's Assault on Civil Liberties*. Gainesville: University Press of Florida, 2014.

Rivera, Rhonda R. "Queer Law: Sexual Orientation Law in the Mid-Eighties Part I." *University of Dayton Law Review* 10, no. 3 (1985): 459–540.

Robson, Ruthann. *Gay Men, Lesbians, and the Law*. New York: Chelsea House, 1997.

"*Romer v. Evans*." Lambda Legal. Accessed September 12, 2018. https://www .lambdalegal.org/in-court/cases/romer-v-evans.

Rosky, Clifford J. "Anti-Gay Curriculum Laws." *Utah Law Faculty Scholarship* 13 (2017): 1–60. https://dc.law.utah.edu/cgi/viewcontent.cgi?article=1012&context =scholarship.

"Sample Character and Fitness Application." Arizona Court. Accessed September 29, 2017. http://www.azcourts.gov/Portals/26/admis/pdf/SampleCharacterAndFitnes sApplication.pdf.

Schnur, James A. "Closet Crusaders: The Johns Committee and Homophobia, 1956–1965." In *Carryin' On in the Lesbian and Gay South*, edited by John Howard, 132–163. New York: New York University Press, 1997.

Sears, Brad, Nan D. Hunter, and Christy Mallory. "Documenting Discrimination on the Basis of Sexual Orientation and Gender Identity in State Employment." Williams Institute, September 2009. Accessed August 14, 2019. https:// williamsinstitute.law.ucla.edu/research/discrimination/documenting -discrimination-on-the-basis-of-sexual-orientation-and-gender-identity-in-state -employment/.

Sepinuck, Stephen L., and Mary Pat Treuthart, eds. *The Conscience of the Court: Selected Opinions of Justice William J. Brennan, Jr. on Freedom and Equality*. Carbondale: Southern Illinois University Press, 1999.

Siegel, Paul. "Lesbian and Gay Rights as a Free Speech Issue." *Journal of Homosexuality* 21, nos. 1–2 (1991): 203–260. https://doi.org/10.1300/J082v21n01_14.

Sinanovic, Jasmina. "Futures of the Field." CLAGS Center for LGBTQ Studies, March 1, 2013. https://clags.org/articles/futures-of-the-field/.

Smith, Paul. "Justice Kennedy: The Linchpin of the Transformation of Civil Rights for the LGBTQ Community." *SCOTUSblog*, June 28, 2018. https://www .scotusblog.com/2018/06/justice-kennedy-the-linchpin-of-the-transformation-of -civil-rights-for-the-lgbtq-community/.

"Special Verdict Law and Legal Definition." USLegal.com. Accessed September 19, 2017. https://definitions.uslegal.com/s/special-verdict/.

"State Maps of Laws & Policies: Employment." Human Rights Campaign. Accessed February 16, 2019. https://www.hrc.org/state-maps/employment.

"State Religious Freedom Restoration Acts." National Conference of State Legislatures, May 4, 2017. http://www.ncsl.org/research/civil-and-criminal-justice/state -rfra-statutes.aspx.

Steadman, Dan, dir. *Taboo Teaching: A Profile of Missouri Teacher Rodney Wilson*. Los Angeles: Circa 87 Films, 2019. Accessed January 18, 2021. https://youtu.be /sNW4CBpj8HY.

"Summary Judgment." *West's Encyclopedia of American Law*. 2nd ed. Accessed September 11, 2017. http://legal-dictionary.thefreedictionary.com /summary+judgment.

"Suspect Classification." Legal Information Institute. Accessed December 16, 2020. https://www.law.cornell.edu/wex/suspect_classification.

Taylor, Ashley P. "Trump Administration's Definitions of Sex Defy Science." *The Scientist*, October 23, 2018. https://www.the-scientist.com/news-opinion/trump -administrations-definitions-of-sex-defy-science—64993.

Tedeschi, Matt. "Somewhere over the Rainbow? What the *Bostock* Decision Means for the LGBT Community." Prinz Law Firm. Accessed February 13, 2021. https:// www.prinz-lawfirm.com/our-blog/2020/june/somewhere-over-the-rainbow-what -the-bostock-deci/

Tribe, Laurence H. "Lawrence v. Texas: The 'Fundamental Right' that Dare Not Speak Its Name." *Harvard Law Review* 117, no. 6 (April 2004): 1893–1955.

"The Triumph of the Religious Right." *The Economist*, November 11, 2004. https:// www.economist.com/special-report/2004/11/11/the-triumph-of-the-religious-right.

Walker, Harron. "Here's Every State that Requires Schools to Teach LGBTQ+ History." *Out*, August 16, 2019. https://www.out.com/news/2019/8/16/heres-every -state-requires-schools-teach-lgbtq-history.

Walker, Vanessa Siddle. *The Lost Education of Horace Tate: Uncovering the Hidden Heroes Who Fought for Justice in Schools*. New York: New Press, 2018.

Widener, Benjamin E. "Sex Discrimination Includes Sexual Orientation Says the 7th Circuit." *National Law Review*, April 14, 2017. https://www.natlawreview.com /article/sex-discrimination-includes-sexual-orientation-says-7th-circuit.

Wiley, Diane. "Expanding Civil Voir Dire." *Guild Notes* 11 (January/February 1982): 19.

Yoshino, Kenji. *Covering: The Hidden Assault on Our Civil Rights*. New York: Random House, 2006.

———. "The New Equal Protection." *Harvard Law Review* 124 (2011): 747–803. http://harvardlawreview.org/wp-content/uploads/pdfs/vol124_yoshino.pdf.

Zamansky, Stephen. "Colorado's Amendment 2 and Homosexuals' Right to Equal Protection of the Law." *Boston College Law Review* 35, no. 1 (1993): 221–258. https://lawdigitalcommons.bc.edu/cgi/viewcontent.cgi?referer=https://www .google.com/&httpsredir=1&article=1986&context=bclr.

Zimmerman, Jonathan, and Emily Robertson. *The Case for Contention: Teaching Controversial Issues in American Schools*. Chicago: University of Chicago Press, 2017.

Index

About the Authors

KAREN L. GRAVES recently retired from Denison University in Granville, Ohio. She is the author of *And They Were Wonderful Teachers: Florida's Purge of Gay and Lesbian Teachers* and a coeditor of *Inexcusable Omissions: Clarence Karier and the Critical Tradition in History of Education Scholarship*.

MARGARET A. NASH is a professor emerita in the School of Education at the University of California, Riverside. She is the editor of *Women's Higher Education in the United States: New Historical Perspectives* and the author of *Women's Education in the United States, 1780–1840*.

Printed in the United States
by Baker & Taylor Publisher Services